SCHÜLER-LERNKRIMI ENGLISCH

Eiskalte Rache

Laura Montgomery

Compact Verlag

Bisher sind in dieser Reihe erschienen:
- Compact Schüler-Lernkrimi Englisch
- Compact Schüler-Lernkrimi Latein

In der Reihe Lernkrimi sind erschienen:
- Compact Lernkrimi Englisch:
  Grundwortschatz, Aufbauwortschatz, Grammatik, Konversation
- Compact Lernkrimi Englisch GB/US: Grammatik, Konversation
- Compact Lernkrimi Business English: Wortschatz, Konversation
- Compact Lernkrimi Französisch: Grundwortschatz, Grammatik
- Compact Lernkrimi Italienisch: Grundwortschatz, Grammatik
- Compact Lernkrimi Spanisch: Grundwortschatz, Grammatik
- Compact Lernkrimi Deutsch: Grundwortschatz, Grammatik

In der Reihe Lernthriller sind erschienen:
- Compact Lernthriller Englisch:
  Grundwortschatz, Aufbauwortschatz, Grammatik, Konversation

In der Reihe Lernstory Mystery sind erschienen:
- Compact Lernstory Mystery Englisch:
  Grundwortschatz, Aufbauwortschatz

Weitere Titel sind in Vorbereitung.

© 2005 Compact Verlag München
Alle Rechte vorbehalten. Nachdruck, auch auszugsweise,
nur mit ausdrücklicher Genehmigung des Verlages gestattet.
Chefredaktion: Evelyn Boos
Redaktion: Sabine Framing
Fachredaktion: Fiona Cain
Produktion: Wolfram Friedrich
Illustrationen: Sonja Heller
Titelillustration: Karl Knospe
Typographischer Entwurf: Maria Seidel
Umschlaggestaltung: Inga Koch

ISBN 3-8174-7612-4
7276121

Besuchen Sie uns im Internet: www.compactverlag.de

Vorwort

Mit dem neuen, spannenden Compact Schüler-Lernkrimi könnt ihr eure Englischkenntnisse auf schnelle und einfache Weise vertiefen, auffrischen und überprüfen.

Die Freunde Sarah, Justin, Kevin, Simon und Julia erleichtern das Sprachtraining mit Action und Humor. Die fünf und ihre spannenden Erlebnisse rund um ihre neue Band stehen im Mittelpunkt einer zusammenhängenden Story.

Der Krimi wird auf jeder Seite durch abwechslungsreiche und kurzweilige Übungen ergänzt, die das Lernen unterhaltsam und spannend machen.

Prüfe dein Englisch in Lückentexten, Zuordnungs- und Übersetzungsaufgaben, in Buchstabenspielen und Kreuzworträtseln!

Dieses Sprachtraining im handlichen Format bietet mit 70 Übungen die ideale Trainingsmöglichkeit für zwischendurch. Schreibe die Lösungen einfach ins Buch!

Die richtigen Antworten sind in einem eigenen Lösungsteil zusammengefasst. Im Anhang steht außerdem ein Glossar, in dem die schwierigsten Wörter übersetzt sind. Diese sind im Text kursiv markiert.

Und nun kann die Spannung beginnen ...

Viel Spaß und Erfolg!

Inhalt

Lernkrimi 5
Abschlusstest 113
Lösungen 118
Glossar 123

Story

Sarah, Justin, Kevin, Simon und Julia sind begeistert: Ihr Lieblingslehrer Mr Sharp wählt sie als Musiker für eine neue Band aus und sie werden an einem Bandwettbewerb teilnehmen! Der Spaß beim Komponieren des ersten eigenen Songs und bei den Proben schweißt die "Sneakers" zusammen.

Allerdings stehen ihnen unerwartete Komplikationen bevor: Ihr Song für den Wettbewerb muss brandneu sein – daher verpflichten sich die Bandmitglieder zu strengem Stillschweigen. Als ihr Lied "Secret" jedoch im Internet auftaucht und als Raubkopie in der Schule kursiert, ist die Aufregung groß – ihre Teilnahme am Bandwettbewerb ist gefährdet!

Wer hat eine der CDs mit dem geheimen Song geklaut und warum will der Täter den "Sneakers" schaden? Verdächtige gibt es jede Menge. Viele Mitschüler sind neidisch, weil sie selbst nicht für die Band ausgewählt wurden. Andere sind enttäuscht – Sarahs beste Freudin Karen ist sauer, weil Sarah ihre Zeit nur noch mit der Band verbringt. Auch Al, ein guter Freund von Mr Sharp, den sie bei den Aufnahmen im Tonstudio kennen gelernt haben, ist verdächtig: Er scheint sich allzu geschäftstüchtig um die Zukunft der Band zu kümmern ... Ob es den Sneakers bei ihren Nachforschungen gelingt, den Täter zu stellen und ihren Traum vom berühmten Song zu verwirklichen?

Cold Revenge

"Rrrrring!"

Simon jumped when he heard the school bell ring. The loud sound woke him up from a daydream he had been enjoying. Simon had been imagining himself on the stage at a rock concert. In his thoughts hundreds of people were watching him play his guitar. His girlfriend was standing in the first row and smiling at him. He was in the middle of his fantastic guitar solo when the bell brought him back to reality.

In that reality Simon was not a rock star. He was just a teenage school pupil who liked playing the guitar in his free time. And although he was one of the best-looking boys in school, he didn't really have a girlfriend. Instead, the reality was that Simon was late for music class.

"Oh no," he said to himself. "Another boring hour with Mrs Snood." Suddenly he heard the voice of his best friend, Kevin, call to him, "Hey Simon! You're late!" Kevin was running past Simon to the front door of the school.

"I'm late?" Simon answered, as he followed his friend into the building. "You're late too! Old Mrs Snood is going to scream at both of us."

Übung 1: In diesem Textabschnitt sind die Adverbien durcheinander gekommen. Finde heraus, wohin die Adverbien tatsächlich gehören!

The two boys hurried and went (1. slowly) _____ up the stairs and down the corridor to room 363, where Mrs Snood was probably waiting with an angry look on her face. (2. immediately) _____ and (3. quickly) _____ they opened the door of the classroom, hoping that no one would see them walk in. But when they looked at the front of the classroom, they realized that they had been worried for no reason.

Mrs Snood wasn't there. In fact, there was no teacher there at all.

"Simon! Kevin! Come to the front of the room (4. loudly) _____. You're both in very serious trouble!"

The two boys saw Sarah, one of their classmates, standing on Mrs Snood's desk. She was imitating their teacher's voice, speaking (5. quietly) _____. Sarah's head, which was covered with short, bright pink hair, *shook* from side to side as she *pretended* to be very angry with the two late pupils.

"What? *What the heck* is going on here?!" said Kevin.
"It's great, *guys*," Sarah said. "You won't believe it. Mrs Snood is moving to Australia! She's never coming back. We're free!" She pulled a piece of *fabric* out of her pocket that had the symbol for anarchy on it. She held it above her head. Then she jumped off the desk and started running around the room.
"That girl has too much energy," Simon said to Kevin. "I don't …"
Suddenly the classroom door opened behind Simon. He turned around and saw the headmaster's small, black eyes looking at him angrily. Sarah stopped running. All the pupils went to their desks.
"All right, everyone, the party's over," Headmaster Jones said.

Übung 2: Setze die Verben ins Simple Past!

ÜBUNG 2

"I guess someone (1. to tell) _____ you that Mrs Snood has decided to move to Australia to help her sister, who is ill," the headmaster (2. to say) _____.

"Hooray," Sarah said quietly.

"I (3. to hear) _____ that. Anyway, we're all very lucky because Mr Sharp has agreed to teach your music class for the rest of the year."

"Mr Sharp – who's that?" (4. to ask) _____ Simon.

Headmaster Jones (5. to step) _____ away from the door. Behind him stood a tall young man wearing jeans and a black jumper. His straight black hair, which normally (6. to come) _____ down to his shoulders, was pulled back into a ponytail. He (7. to smile) _____ at the teenagers in the room.

"This is Mr Sharp's first teaching job, so be nice," Headmaster Jones said. Then he looked at Mr Sharp and added, "They're all yours."

He walked out of the room and closed the door. Mr Sharp went to the front of the classroom. He looked at the pupils for a few seconds and said, "So, *what's up?*"

Before anyone could answer, the door opened again and a pretty

blonde girl wearing a flowery dress *burst* into the room and started talking quickly.

"Mrs Snood, I've got a note from my mum that says I was … Wait. Where's Mrs Snood?" she asked. "And who's the *cute guy*? He's really *fit*."

"Janet," *whispered* Simon, "that '*cute guy*' is our new teacher, Mr Sharp. Now you'd better sit down and be quiet before he *punishes* us all."

"Oh, he wouldn't *punish* us – would you, Mr Sharp? You seem like you're too cool for the rules," said Janet.

"Well, there are some rules that you have to take very seriously," Mr Sharp said. The pupils *frowned*. "But," he added, "there are some rules that were made to be broken."

"*Damn*, this *guy* really is cool," Kevin said.

"Well … what's your name?"

"Kevin."

"Well, Kevin, I'm not so cool that I'll let you use words like that in my classroom. But I think you'll find that I'm much more *laid-back* than old Mrs Snood."

The pupils laughed. They spent the next thirty minutes telling Mr Sharp their names and talking about what they'd been doing in class for the past few months. They explained that each of the pupils played a different instrument. But recently Mrs Snood had been teaching them about classical music.

ÜBUNG 3

Übung 3: Übersetze die musikalischen Instrumente und enträtsele das Lösungswort!

1. Trompete   _ _ _ _ ☐ _ _
2. Gitarre   _ _ ☐ _ _ _

3. Saxophon   – ☐ _ _ _ _
4. Geige   _ _ _ _ _ ☐
5. Orgel   ☐ _ _ _ _

Lösung: _ _ _ _ _

"How boring!" said Sarah. "I kept waiting for the day when she'd stop talking about that stupid *stuff* and start talking about real music. You know, good *stuff* like punk and ska."

"Yeah, but it could have been worse," said Kevin. "Old Snood could have made us listen to jazz music."

"Hey! Don't say anything bad about jazz. Jazz is great. You're just too dumb to understand it."

Most of the pupils were surprised to hear the voice of Julia, a sweet but *shy* girl who didn't talk much. Usually she sat low in her chair, silently looking at everyone through her glasses. But now she sat up straight and looked at Simon with a strong, angry expression on her face.

Julia played the saxophone and was a huge fan of jazz music.

"Just because you can sing and play a few simple songs on your silly guitar, you think you know everything about music," Julia said to Simon.

Simon's face turned red and he said nothing. Although everyone at school liked him, he was actually quite *insecure*. Yes, he was very good at sports and girls often flirted with him. But Simon often worried that he wasn't very good at making the thing that was most important to him – music.

"Julia has a point," said Mr Sharp. "No kind of music is better than the other. They're just different. That's why someone like Sarah might like punk, Julia might like jazz, or – Kevin, what kind of music do you like the most?"

Übung 4: Vervollständige die Sätze mit a, an oder the!

1. The instrument Simon plays is _____ guitar.

2. Would you like to hear _____ interesting song?

3. That's _____ best song I've ever heard!

4. Could you say that _____ bit slower, please?

5. Kevin is _____ very nice person.

6. I've been waiting here for _____ hour.

Kevin answered, "Oh, I like anything I can listen to while I'm skateboarding. Anything fast with a *wicked* bass, because I play the bass, and I …"

"I'm a singer," Janet *interrupted*. "I sing pop songs. That's my real talent. Mrs Snood always wanted me to play the *tambourine*, but the *tambourine* is the instrument that *backing singers* play. I was born to be a solo singing star!"

"That's good to know, Janet," Mr Sharp said with a smile. The school bell rang and the pupils began collecting their things. "Be ready to talk about classical music again in our next lesson, everyone!"

Simon said, "Oh, come on, Mr Sharp! You said you were going to be more fun than stupid old Mrs Snood!"

"Simon," he answered, "you can become a great musician only if you understand the masters who have come before you. But I promise that we'll have a lot of fun in other ways. See you on Thursday, everyone!"

Two days later, the pupils returned to room 363 for their second music lesson with their new teacher. Although they talked about classical music during the 45-minute lesson, the pupils had a great time and laughed a lot. Somehow the subject seemed much more interesting when Mr Sharp talked about it.

"Have a good weekend," Mr Sharp said at the end of the lesson. "And don't forget – I'm going to have a nice surprise for you next week. Bye!"

As Simon walked out of the classroom, he *whispered* to Sarah, "I wonder what it will be!"

"*Chill out*, Simon," she said. "We'll find out soon enough."

On Tuesday morning the kids found out what Mr Sharp's surprise was. When they arrived at the entrance to their classroom they saw a big sign on the door:

WANTED:
Five *brilliant* musicians to form
the coolest band in the school!
Lots of hard work –
but you could become famous!
***Auditions* will be in room 363 this afternoon at 4.00 pm.**
Only the best five will be chosen.

Übung 5: Schreibe die Uhrzeiten in Zahlen!

1. quarter past ten in the morning   *10.15 am*

2. five minutes to nine in the afternoon   _____

3. three twenty-seven in the afternoon   _____

4. ten past eleven in the morning   _____

5. noon　　　　　　　　　　＿＿＿＿＿＿＿＿＿＿

6. half past one in the afternoon　　＿＿＿＿＿＿＿＿＿＿

7. eight forty-three in the morning　＿＿＿＿＿＿＿＿＿＿

"You want the best? Here I am," said Janet.

Sarah's nose piercing sparkled as she shouted, "Wow! I'll finally get a chance to show what a great drummer I am! Everyone *protect* your ears – it's going to get loud!"

Julia had a huge smile on her face but said nothing.

The kids ran into the classroom and formed a circle around Mr Sharp. Everyone shouted and asked questions at the same time.

"Which instruments will be in the band?"

"When will the band have *rehearsals*?"

"Are *auditions* only for the people in this class?"

"How will we become famous?"

Mr Sharp told the pupils to be quiet and then said, "The *auditions* are open to anyone in the school. Of course we'll need a guitarist and drummer, but the other instruments will depend on who the best musicians are. *Rehearsals* will be after school, because this is a special, extra project." He continued talking and explained that he wanted to form the band because there was a national teen band *competition*. Bands from around the country were invited to write a song, *record* it, and send it in for the *competition*. The band with the best song would win £5,000 and a chance to get a *recording contract* with a famous English record company.

"*I'm gonna be* a rock star, I just know it!" said Kevin.

"That's fantastic; that's my greatest dream," said Simon. "I would love to be in a recording studio, playing my guitar – and maybe even singing."

"We could sing a duet together, Simon," said Janet, flirting with him. "Wouldn't that be romantic? You could come to my house and we could rehearse in my room."

Simon's face turned red. He knew that Janet liked him. But he had never felt attracted to her. He thought she needed too much *attention*. He wanted a girl who was happy with the way she was. But he said nothing, because he didn't want to hurt Janet's feelings.

Übung 6: In diesem Gitternetz sind fünf Farben versteckt. Findest du sie alle?

T	E	N	G	I	W
A	S	G	R	E	H
B	L	U	E	Z	I
M	O	R	E	D	T
O	R	A	N	G	E

Later that afternoon around 25 pupils from the school went to the band *auditions*. Each pupil had to go into room 363 alone and play a song for Mr Sharp. Some kids brought their own instruments. Others used the instruments in the music classroom.

While waiting for her chance to play a song on her saxophone, Julia saw a boy named Justin walk out of the *audition* room. She was surprised. Everyone at school knew that Justin was a computer *genius* – but no one had known that he was interested in music too.

"Hey, Justin," Julia said. "I thought you spent all your time playing with your computer and writing computer programs that do your homework for you. What instrument do you play?"

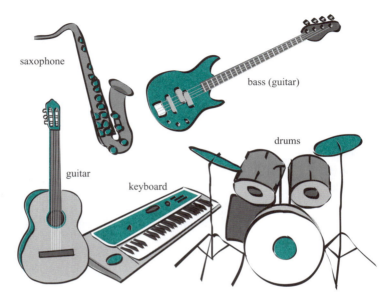

Justin answered, "Well, a computer *keyboard* isn't the only keyboard I like to play with. I've been taking piano lessons since I was four years old. So I decided to *audition* by playing the electric keyboard."

"Oh," Julia said, "so there's a secret side of Justin, is there?"

"I think we all have our own secret side – even you, Julia," Justin said. "Well, I have to go. Good luck!"

As Justin walked away Julia heard Mr Sharp call her name. She picked up her saxophone, took a deep breath, and walked into room 363 for her *audition*.

Two days later a small piece of paper hung on the door to Mr Sharp's classroom. On it was written: "Thank you to everyone who took part in the auditions on Tuesday. This school is filled with musical talent, and the final decision was very difficult." After that were listed five names:

Guitar and *vocals*: Simon Smith
Drums: Sarah Patton
Bass: Kevin Jones
Saxophone and *vocals*: Julia Monaghan
Keyboard: Justin Roe

The pupils formed a *crowd* around the door.
"Yes!" screamed Sarah. "I'm the drummer! I was so worried because my ex-boyfriend was at the *auditions* too. He's the person who taught me how to play the drums. But he's a perfect idiot about everything else. He'll be so angry that Mr Sharp chose me." She smiled.

Übung 7: Welches Wort ist das „schwarze Schaf"? Unterstreiche das nicht in die Reihe passende Wort!

1. table, chair, desk, room
2. piano, music, flute, violin
3. teacher, pupil, class, headmaster
4. big, huge, tall, thin
5. corridor, kitchen, bedroom, radio
6. lesson, hour, minute, second
7. sick, ill, flu, unwell
8. angry, mad, glad, annoyed

"I can't believe he chose me for *vocals*," said Simon.
"I can believe he chose you," Kevin said. "But I can't believe that he

wants Julia, the quietest girl in school, to sing." He *pointed to* Julia using the skateboard he was holding in his hands.

Simon said, "I heard Julia through the door when she *auditioned*. She's got a fantastic voice. You'll be surprised. And she's a great sax player too. I mean, I'm not a fan of jazz, but she really seems to know what she's doing."

Janet had been standing at the back of the *crowd*, smiling. She had simply *assumed* that Mr Sharp had chosen her to be the band's lead singer. But now that she heard Simon and Kevin talking, she pushed her way to the front of the *crowd* to see the list on the door.

"Wha... What? WHAT?! There must have been a mistake. Where is my name? I can't believe that! The list is supposed to say 'Lead *vocals*: Janet Starr'. Where's Mr Sharp? I want an explanation!" she screamed.

"I can give you an explanation," Sarah said sarcastically. "Your voice stinks, *darling*. I heard you sing a version of some pop song for your *audition*. But I didn't even know what song it was, because you were so terrible."

Janet ran towards Sarah, "Take that back! I was born to be a star!" She stopped and turned towards the others. "But instead, stupid Julia and that computer *geek*, Justin, stole my place. *What about* our beautiful duet, Simon?"

Simon looked at the floor and said nothing.

"I understand now, Simon! You're one of the singers. You're probably happy that you get to sing and I don't!"

Janet *shook* her blonde hair dramatically and covered her face with her hands. Suddenly she pulled her hands away and ran down the corridor. The other pupils in the *crowd*, the ones who hadn't been chosen to be in the band, started walking away too. A boy and a girl stood in front of the door for a few more moments. They both looked very shocked and sad. But finally they left too.

Übung 8: Setze das richtige Fragewort ein!

1. _____ are you doing this afternoon?
2. _____ do you enjoy more – swimming or running?
3. _____ does the film start? I don't want to be late!
4. _____ is she? I've never met her before.
5. _____ big is your family's new house?
6. _____ is your name?
7. _____ is your sister's birthday?

Soon Simon, Kevin, Sarah, Julia and Justin were alone. Kevin was standing in front of the door to room 363 and he jumped when he heard a noise behind him. He turned around and saw Mr Sharp's left eye looking at him through a small opening in the door.

"Is the storm finished yet?" Mr Sharp asked. He opened the door wider. "I wanted to wait until all the other pupils left. I didn't want to *embarrass* the rest of you." He opened the door completely and took a step backwards. "Come inside. We have a lot to talk about."

The five chosen teenagers walked into the room and Mr Sharp closed the door behind him. "Starting now," he said, "everything that we talk about in this room is *top secret*. Of course, not the things we talk about during our regular music lessons. I mean anything that we talk about in the afternoons after school – during our band meetings and *rehearsals*. Do you understand?"

Everyone nodded. But then Simon looked at Sarah and said, "Hey, did you hear that, *big mouth*? Secret. Do you really understand what that means?"

"*Shut up*, Si-monster," Sarah said. "I might be loud, but that doesn't mean that I can't keep my mouth shut about things that are really important."

Mr Sharp continued. "There's a reason for making everything such a big secret."

Although they knew that the other pupils in the school had already gone home, Justin, Sarah, Simon, Kevin and Julia moved closer to Mr Sharp. Their teacher also started speaking more quietly.

"As I explained a few days ago there's a national teen band *competition*. It's being organized by a famous English record company. They're looking for the best new, young band in England. To take part in the *competition*, each band has to write an original song. So we can't simply play our own version of a song that someone else wrote. But there's a special rule that every band has to follow. The song for the *competition* has to be brand new. That means the song can't be *released* before the *competition*. The people at the record company want to be sure that they have exclusive rights to the song. That's why I think we should keep everything a secret. I think you *guys* are really talented. And I don't want anything to destroy your chances of success."

Übung 9: Welche der Übersetzungen stimmt? Kreuze die richtige Lösung an!

1. Es gibt bestimmte Regeln.
    a) ☐ There are certain rules.
    b) ☐ It gives certain rules.

2. Die Band hat eine Chance bekommen.
    a) ☐ The band got a chance.
    b) ☐ The band became a chance.

3. Sie will am Wettbewerb teilnehmen.
   a) ☐ She will take part in the *competition*.
   b) ☐ She wants to take part in the *competition*.

4. Sie sind sehr an Musik interessiert.
   a) ☐ They are very interesting in music.
   b) ☐ They are very interested in music.

5. Justin spielt seit 12 Jahren Klavier.
   a) ☐ Justin has played the piano since 12 years.
   b) ☐ Justin has played the piano for 12 years.

"I agree," said Kevin. "I don't want anything to come between me and five thousand pounds!"
"You mean one thousand pounds," said Justin. "If we win, we each get part of the prize money."
"Okay," Mr Sharp said. "Now that you all understand what's happening, I'll leave the five of you alone for a while."
"Why?" asked Julia. "Do we have to start writing the song now?"
Mr Sharp answered, "No, Julia, not yet. But you do have to do something almost as important. You have to choose a band name! Good luck! I'll see you all tomorrow." He walked out.
As soon as Mr Sharp closed the door, Simon said, "Let's try to do this quickly."
"Yeah, I have to meet some friends in the park to go skateboarding," said Kevin.
"And I have to meet my best friend, Karen. We're going to a punk concert this evening," Sarah said. "I think we should call ourselves The Anarchists!"
Justin said, "But I'm not an anarchist. I always follow the rules."
"You're so boring, Justin!" Sarah said.

"I am not! I think The *Fabulous* Five sounds better," Justin said.
"I like the name The Winners," said Simon. He looked around at the others to see if they agreed. "With a name like that, there's no way we can lose the *competition*!"
"The Winners? You loser. That's a stupid name," Sarah laughed.
They were quiet for a while and tried to think of a good name. Kevin *scratched* his head. Sarah bit her fingernails.

Übung 10: Beantworte die Fragen zum Text!

1. What subject does Mr Sharp teach?

   _____

2. What instrument does Kevin play?

   _____

3. How much money could the band win?

   _____

4. What kind of music does Julia like?

   _____

5. What band name does Justin like?

   _____

"I have an idea," said Julia. "Mr Sharp said we have to keep this project a secret. So why don't we call ourselves The Sneakers?"
"That sounds cool," said Justin. "It combines the verb *'to sneak'* and the American word for *trainers – sneakers*."
"Yeah, cool," said Simon.

Kevin and Sarah agreed too. The five teenagers picked up their rucksacks and walked out of the classroom. When they reached the front door, Sarah said to the others, "See you tomorrow, Sneakers!"

"Careful – don't say that so loud!" Justin said. "Everthing about our band is supposed to be a secret, remember?"

The Sneakers said goodbye to each other and walked away in different directions.

The next day Justin arrived at school very early in the morning. Mr Sharp found him waiting in front of the door to his classroom. There were no other pupils in the school yet. Justin seemed a bit nervous.

"Good morning, Justin," Mr Sharp said. "Is something wrong? You seem to be worried about something."

"Well, Mr Sharp," Justin answered, "I wanted to know if you might be able to do something for me."

"What is it?"

"You see, I would like to know if I could transfer into your music class. I mean, everyone else in the band is in the class, and I don't want to miss anything just because I'm not there. I know our *rehearsals* are after school. But I'm worried that I will be left out if I'm not in the class too."

Mr Sharp thought for a moment. "I understand how you feel, Justin. But the school year started three weeks ago. Would your other teacher allow you to just stop coming to her class because you wanted to join mine?"

Justin answered, "I don't think it would be a problem. I have my computer programming lesson at the same time as your music lesson. But the computer class is too easy for me. I've taught myself a lot about computers at home. Learning about computers is one of my favourite hobbies. So I think my teacher would understand if I told her that I wanted to transfer to a different class."

Übung 11: *Ordne den passenden zweiten Teil jedes Wortes zu! Trage die richtige Nummer in das Kästchen ein!*

1. girl-
2. class-
3. head-
4. week-
5. skate-
6. some-
7. finger-

☐ -one
☐ -end
☐ -friend
☐ -board
☐ -room
☐ -nail
☐ -master

Mr Sharp looked at Justin carefully. "Well, if your computer teacher says it's okay, then it's okay with me too."
Justin held his fist up in the air and shouted, "Yes!" Then he realized how excited he was and said in a quieter voice, "I mean, thanks, Mr Sharp. This means a lot to me." At that moment the school bell rang. Justin said goodbye and walked away.
In the corridor he saw his friend, Joe. Joe had *auditioned* to be in the band too. He had wanted to be the band's guitarist.
"I'm glad you got chosen to be in the band, Justin," Joe said. "But tell me – why did Mr Sharp want to make the band?"
Justin smiled and said, "Well, we're not really sure yet."
"Come on, you can tell me," Joe said. But Justin was quiet. "Fine. I understand. You can't tell your old friend Joe your big secret. Fine. See you later." He walked away.
After school that day the five members of The Sneakers met in room 363 for their first band *rehearsal*. Mr Sharp was waiting for them.
"Hi everyone. You're all probably very excited about playing music and working on our song."
"You know I am," said Sarah with a lot of enthusiasm. "Where are my drums? I'm ready to rock!"

Kevin added, "Me too. I have some great ideas for the song."

Mr Sharp *interrupted*, "I'm happy to hear that. But before you start rehearsing, I think you *guys* should do some *research*."

"What do you mean?" asked Justin.

"I think you should go to the music shop on Wood Street," said Mr Sharp. "*Check out* some of the CDs they've got there. Experiment. Try listening to music you don't normally listen to. For example, Julia could show Sarah some of her favourite jazz albums. Simon, you could help Justin listen to some good rock 'n' roll music. And Sarah, you could introduce Kevin to the world of punk rock. What do you think?"

Simon said, "I would prefer playing my guitar. But shopping for CDs is fun too. Let's go, *guys*. See you later, Mr Sharp."

Übung 12: Schreibe die Wörter in Großbuchstaben um!

1. Change a letter in PEG to make a word for a body part. _____
2. Change a letter in SHOE to make a word for a place where you buy things. _____
3. Change a letter in WOOL to make a word for what a tree is made of. _____
4. Change a letter in THING to make a word for what you do to find an answer. _____
5. Change a letter in SELL to make a word for something that rings. _____
6. Change a letter in ROSE to make a word for a part of your face. _____

The pupils left the school and started walking down the street in the direction of Wood Street. Kevin jumped onto his skateboard and did some tricks on the *pavement* as the group walked. His *shaggy* brown hair hung in front of his eyes and the others wondered how he could see what he was doing. It was a beautiful, sunny afternoon. No one said much as they walked.

When the group walked into Music 4 U, the music shop on Wood Street, the *guy* who worked there looked up from his computer and looked at them. He was two or three years older than they were. He had black hair and very white skin and wore a long leather jacket, although it was quite warm inside the shop. He was wearing a big pair of *headphones*, but took them off when the five teenagers entered the shop. They could hear loud heavy metal music coming from the *headphones*.

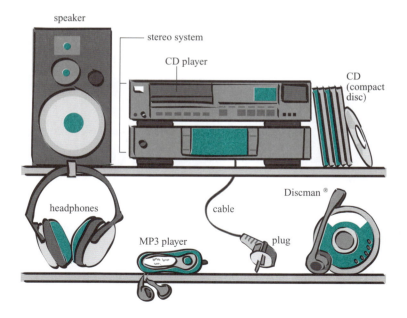

"Can I help you?" he asked them.

"No, thanks. We just want to look around for a while," said Simon.

Justin took an album from the punk section. Kevin chose a jazz CD. Julia asked Sarah which punk album she should listen to. Simon took a CD from the surf rock section, which Kevin had *recommended*. Finally, Sarah had to choose an album.

"What should I buy? There aren't any types of music left," she said.

"I could *recommend* something," said Justin.

"Oh, no," Sarah said. "I don't want to listen to classical piano music. No one can make me believe that that is good, fun music."

"Well, I really wanted to tell you about a great hip-hop group I like," Justin said.

"Did you just say hip-hop?" said Kevin. "A computer *freak* who likes hip-hop? I can't believe it. This is a big surprise."

"You shouldn't be surprised," said Justin. "There are a lot of things about me you don't know. I have a lot of different interests." He smiled. After looking around for a few more minutes, the *youngsters* went to the front of the store to pay for their CDs.

"This is a lot of music," said the *guy* working there, in his strange, deep voice. "Are you all in a band or something?"

The band members looked at each other nervously. Mr Sharp had told them to keep information about the band a secret.

"We're … um … just interested in music," Simon said. They quickly paid and left the shop.

During the weekend each of the band members listened to their new music. Simon played his guitar for a while and thought about what The Sneakers' song should be about. Sarah made her parents crazy by playing her drums all weekend long. Julia spent her weekend doing the same thing she usually did. She played her saxophone, read books, and wrote some *poetry*. Kevin played his bass at home and tried to add some jazz sounds to the things he played.

*Übung 13: Vervollständige die Sätze mit **their, there** oder **they're**!*

1. The teenagers like music. _____ in a band!

2. _____ are some really cool CDs here.

3. I want to go _____ at the weekend.

4. They talked about _____ favourite music styles.

5. The band members worked on _____ song.

6. _____ all working very hard.

On Tuesday afternoon The Sneakers had their first band *rehearsal*. After their school lessons were finished, Justin, Simon, Kevin, Julia and Sarah met in Mr Sharp's room.

"I hope you all enjoyed experimenting with different kinds of music over the weekend," said Mr Sharp. "I think that will help you understand each other better. And it should help you to work together."

"Yeah," said Kevin. "I'd like to show you all some ideas for a song that I was thinking about."

"I'd love to hear about it."

Mr Sharp and the pupils looked around the room, wondering who had spoken. They wanted to find out where that girl's voice had come from. Then they all saw a short girl with black hair standing at the door. She smiled and took a few steps into the room.

"What's she doing here?!" shouted Sarah. "You're not allowed in here. This is a private meeting."

"Be nice, Sarah," said Mr Sharp. Then he said to the girl, "Hi Susie. Can I help you with something?"

"Well," Susie said in a nice, sweet voice, "I think I left my pen in here during the *auditions*." She walked to the desk where Kevin was sitting. She looked at Kevin and smiled sweetly. "Have you seen my pen, Kevin?"

Kevin's eyes opened wide with surprise. Was Susie flirting with him? He had talked to her last week while they were waiting to *audition* for the band. She wanted to be the band's keyboard player, but Mr Sharp didn't choose her.

He smiled back at Susie and said, "Um … I … no. I mean, I don't know where your pen is. But you can have one of mine, if you want to." He reached down into his rucksack and tried to find a pen to give to her. He found one and stood up to give it to her.

Susie stepped close to Kevin and *whispered* into his ear, "Thanks, Kevin." Kevin gave her a big, silly smile.

Übung 14: Finde die gesuchten Begriffe heraus und trage sie ins Kreuzworträtsel ein!

1. something loud that you hear
2. someone who learns in school
3. the thing in the sky that gives light
4. something you use to write
5. what you do when you're happy

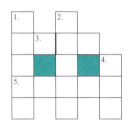

Justin coughed. "I don't want to break up this lovely scene," he said. "But we have a lot to do. I don't want to be impolite, Susie, but that's the way it is. So please leave now."

Susie laughed, "Sorry. I'll let you all return to your 'private meeting' – whatever that is." She looked at Kevin again and then walked out of the room.

"What a *freak*," Sarah said after Susie closed the door.

"Let's not worry about her," said Simon seriously. "We have a lot of work to do. Kevin, let's hear what you've done so far."

Kevin put his hands on his face. He could feel that his face was still warm – and probably red too. "Oh," he said, "maybe someone else wants to go first. Justin?"

Justin jumped up happily. He was glad that Kevin and the other band members were starting to accept him. "Sure," he said. "I've got something I'd like you all to hear." Justin opened his rucksack and pulled out a small laptop computer. He turned the computer on and started pressing *buttons* on the *keyboard*. He explained, "I have a program on my computer that lets me mix different songs together." Justin pressed another *button* and the room filled with music. Everyone listened to the sounds for several seconds. Sarah started hitting a desk with her hands, as though she were playing the drums. "I like it!" she said.

Soon the music stopped. "I didn't have time to do more," Justin said. "That's really interesting, Justin," said Mr Sharp.

"It sounded a little too fast," Simon said. "I think our song should have more emotion. I can't sing something if it doesn't make me feel something."

Übung 15: *In diesen Sätzen sind die Wörter durcheinander gekommen. Wie lauten die Sätze richtig? Trage sie mit Satzzeichen und richtiger Groß- und Kleinschreibung ein!*

1. lot has Sarah energy a of

Sarah has a lot of energy.

2. this do song like you?

3. with likes computers playing Justin

_____

4. secret everything a is why?

_____

5. Janet not band is the in

_____

"Don't be such a baby, Simon," said Sarah. Her voice sounded sarcastic. "The only thing I need to feel when I'm playing is energy!"

"I agree with Simon," said Julia. "People need to feel something emotional when they listen to a song. That's what makes music great." She picked up her saxophone and *licked* her lips. She raised the instrument to her mouth and started playing a beautiful, slow, sad song. Everyone else stood or sat quietly and listened to the music coming from Julia's sax. It seemed like she was putting all of her emotions into the song. Love and hate, happiness and sadness. Two minutes later she stopped playing.

"Wow," said Simon.

"That was fantastic," Justin agreed.

Mr Sharp stood up and walked to the front of the room. "This is a really exciting mix of styles and ideas. Let's try to bring some of them together. Get your instruments, everyone. Let's start writing a song!"

Two hours later Mr Sharp looked at his watch. It was getting late.

"All right, *guys*. I think that's enough for today," he said.

"But Mr Sharp," said Simon, "we were just getting started! There's still so much to do!"

"Don't worry, Simon," Mr Sharp's voice was friendly and understanding. "We still have a few more weeks to rehearse. And after that we will have enough time to *record* the song too. Today was your first *rehearsal*. No band is perfect after only one *rehearsal*!" Simon smiled because he realized that Mr Sharp was right.

> **Übung 16:** *Wähle das passende Wort für jeden Satz aus und unterstreiche es!*
>
> 1. There were fewer/less people at the *audition* than they expected.
> 2. Sorry, I haven't got some/any money.
> 3. If they win the *competition*, they'll get a nice price/prize.
> 4. She wanted to tell/say him a secret.
> 5. I put on/wore my jacket before I left the house.
> 6. His father learned/taught him how to read.
> 7. I had to work until/for five o'clock.
> 8. Don't worry on/about her.

Julia was excited too. As she put her sax into its case, she thought about standing on a stage and playing in front of hundreds of people. But she was a bit nervous too. She didn't even know that she had a good singing voice till Mr Sharp chose her to be one of the band's singers. What would the others think?

As Sarah left room 363, she started biting her fingernails again. She did that whenever she was excited about something. She was filled with nervous energy. It was especially difficult for her to keep the band's work a secret. She had never been very good at keeping secrets. But she knew that she had to do the right thing. She wanted to become a famous rock star. So she decided at that moment to put all her energy into her drumming. People would find out the band's secret plans when they won the *competition*, Sarah thought. Till then, she would keep her mouth closed.

Übung 17: Bilde Sätze mit dem Komparativ!

1. village/town (small)

A village is smaller than a town.

2. car/bicycle (expensive)

_____

3. ocean/lake (deep)

_____

4. hip-hop music/classical music (cool)

_____

5. tree/bush (tall)

_____

6. sofa/chair (big)

_____

Every day for the next two weeks, The Sneakers met in room 363 after school for *rehearsals*. They wrote the song *bit by bit*. Each of the band members had a chance to add something special and personal to the song. After the song was finished, they were all surprised by the crazy mix of musical styles it had. But the song was good! They knew it. And Mr Sharp thought so too.

"I have to say I was worried for a while at the beginning," Mr Sharp said at the beginning of the third week of *rehearsals*. "You all like different things, and I wasn't sure if you could combine them all in one song. But it's *mega*." He was quiet for a minute. Then he said, "But there's something missing."

"What?" asked Sarah. "This song rocks!"
"Yes, it does," said Mr Sharp. "But you still need to write the words for the song."
The pupils looked at each other. What should they sing about?
"I've been working on something," Julia said quietly. Everyone turned to look at her. "I write *poetry* sometimes. I think I have a poem that would fit with the music we've written."
"What's it called?" asked Justin.
"It's called 'Secret'. I was thinking about our band and about this secret project. Then I thought about how people react when they have to keep a special secret. So I wrote the poem about someone who tells a secret to other people. It's about friendship, *trust*, anger and *revenge*. But you might think it's silly," Julia said.
"Silly? Anything that's about *revenge* is cool," said Simon. "Let's hear it."
Julia read the poem. She almost sang it, using the melody from the song The Sneakers had written. When she finished, everyone *clapped*.

Übung 18: Unterstreiche die sechs Sätze, die inhaltlich nicht zum Text passen!

The Sneakers spent their third week of *rehearsals* adding Julia's text to the song. They jumped when the balloon exploded. The *rehearsals* were long. Kevin didn't have much time for skateboarding. Justin had to miss many of his piano lessons. But the five teenagers all believed that this project was more important than anything else. They were tired and stressed. Kevin loved to eat chicken and potatoes. But they knew they had to work hard till the song was perfect. It's nice when the weather is sunny.

After two more weeks of hard work, the song was ready. Not many people are on holiday. In only a month and a half the five teenagers had been changed from a group of normal pupils into a real band. And more than that, they had written a song that could win them £5,000. She works in a factory.

At the end of The Sneakers' last *rehearsal* on Friday afternoon, Mr Sharp asked the group, "Will you all have time to *record* the song tomorrow? We have to send in the song for the *competition* on Wednesday. I went to the cinema yesterday."

All the band members said yes.

"Then we'll meet tomorrow morning at 10 o'clock."

"Will we *record* the song here, in room 363?" asked Julia.

"No," Mr Sharp answered. "I've got a surprise for you all. We'll meet here in the morning. But then I'll take you to the place where we'll *record* the song."

Suddenly Simon turned around and looked at the door. "Did you hear that?" he asked. "I thought I heard a noise. I think someone is standing outside the classroom." No one said anything. Simon ran to the door and pulled it open. The corridor was empty.

"Stop worrying so much, Simon," Kevin said. "Just *chill out*. No one is listening to our conversations."

Übung 19: Ordne die Buchstaben zu einem sinnvollen Wort!

On Saturday morning the (1. twerahe) _____ was sunny and nice. Kevin walked down the (2. resett) _____ in a white T-shirt, a pair of baggy (3. jsena) _____ and an old pair of blue *trainers*. He carried his skateboard in his right (4. dnha) _____. He wore a baseball cap to keep the hair out of his (5. syee) _____. He didn't want his hair to get in the way when he played the bass (6. arelt) _____ in the day. Kevin was enjoying feeling the sun on his (7. afec) _____ while he walked down the street. Suddenly he heard someone calling his (8. eman) _____.

"Kevin! Kevin! Wait!"
He turned around and saw Janet running towards him. "Where are you going, Kevin?" she asked with a smile.
"Oh, I'm just going to meet … I mean, I'm going skateboarding. I'm meeting some skateboarding friends at the school building," Kevin answered nervously. He was so excited that Janet was interested in him. But he didn't want to tell Janet that the band planned to *record* their song today.
"Skateboarding? So early in the morning? That's strange," she said. Kevin didn't want to tell her anything about the band's plans. So he answered, "No. I don't want you to see me fall down if I make a mistake." He tried to laugh.
Janet *frowned*, "Oh, that's a pity. At least let me walk with you, okay?" When they reached the school, Janet said goodbye. Kevin was happy that he didn't have to tell her the truth. He met the rest of the band in room 363. Then they all went out the back door of the school with Mr Sharp.
"Get in my *van*, everyone," Mr Sharp said. He led them to a big white *van* with flames on its side. The excited teenagers got into the *van*.

When they got out again fifteen minutes later they were in the next town, standing in front of a building. On the building was a sign that said 'Sam's Studios'.

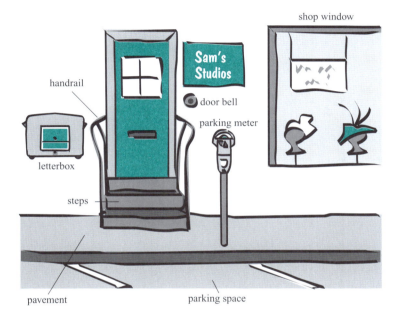

"Wow, that's a professional recording studio! This is great, Mr Sharp!" Sarah said. "But isn't it expensive to *record* a song in a real studio?"

Mr Sharp smiled. "I have another secret for you all – I own this studio. Before I started teaching, I bought this place to help some friends who are in bands. Now I work here at the weekend sometimes. My business partner, Al, works here during the week. But this weekend I'm helping a fantastic young band to *record* their first single!"

The pupils laughed. "Thanks Mr Sharp!" they said together.

Übung 20: Sind die folgenden Aussagen richtig? Markiere mit richtig ✔ oder falsch –!

1. Simon thought someone was listening outside room 363. ☐
2. Kevin wanted to tell Janet about the band's plans. ☐
3. Janet will help The Sneakers *record* their song. ☐
4. The Sneakers are *recording* their song in room 363. ☐
5. The Sneakers rode on Mr Sharp's motorcycle. ☐
6. Mr Sharp works at his studio at the weekend. ☐

They went inside and found their instruments in the studio. As the band was getting ready to start *recording*, Simon saw something black move past the window.

"What was that?" Simon asked. He moved towards the window.

"You're crazy," said Kevin. "This is the second time you've seen or heard something that wasn't there."

Simon didn't get a chance to explain what he had seen. Maybe he was crazy, he thought. But he decided to forget about it for a while. For two hours The Sneakers played and played. Justin's hands hurt from playing the keyboard. Julia's fingers were tired from playing her sax. Kevin thought he would scream if he had to play the song one more time. Finally, Mr Sharp said, "Okay. I think we've got it!"

"Yes, you've really got it," said another man's voice. At the door stood a big, fat man with grey hair. He was smiling and rubbing his hands together. "Where did you find these kids, Sam? They're great."

Mr Sharp said to the man, "Hi, Al. These are my pupils – Kevin, Sarah, Simon, Julia and Justin. I'm helping them *record* a song for a national *competition*." Then he looked at the band and said, "This is my business partner, Al."

"Nice to meet you," Al said. "Why don't you all forget about that *competition*? I could help you *record* a whole album. I've got a lot of *connections*. I know a *guy* at a big record company. He would pay a lot of money for this kind of music."

The Sneakers didn't know what to say. Mr Sharp answered for them.

"No, thanks, Al," he said. "They're not professionals. At least not yet. Let us do this *competition*. You have other projects."

Al said, "But I'd really like to help this band. They're good. This is a good chance for me … I mean, for us to make a lot of money."

"These kids are talented enough," Mr Sharp smiled. "I don't think The Sneakers will need help to become famous." Then he said to the band, "You can all go home now and enjoy the rest of the weekend."

The pupils returned to school the next week after a nice, relaxing weekend. On Tuesday after school Mr Sharp told the band that the song was ready. He stood in front of them holding one CD in his left hand and five CDs in his right hand. He raised his left hand.

"Here is the master copy of the song. I'll take it to the post office when I leave here today. And I'll send it to the people who are organizing the *competition*."

Übung 21: Wähle das passende Wort für jeden Satz aus und unterstreiche es!

1. The band members will see each other again bald/soon.
2. You finished all your homework! You are so good/brave.
3. They hope they will get/become a *recording contract*.
4. Who is the chef/boss of that company?
5. Julia is intelligent and gets perfect marks/notes at school.
6. I just finished reading a fantastic roman/novel!

Then Mr Sharp raised his right hand. "Here are five copies of the song. Each of you gets one. You have to put your CDs in a VERY safe place. If anyone outside the band gets a copy of the song, your chances of winning could be destroyed."

The five pupils understood. Each of them took a copy of the song.

After school Sarah met her best friend, Karen. Karen was a tall girl with long, black hair. While they were talking, Sarah dropped the books she was holding. Her CD, which was inside one of the books, fell out onto the ground.

"What's that?" Karen asked.

"Nothing, nothing," Sarah said quickly.

"Is that what you and your little band have been working on?" asked Karen. "You've been spending all your time with them – I feel like I've lost my best friend. At least let me hear the song, please. You would let me, your BEST friend, hear your first hit song, wouldn't you?"

"I can't," Sarah said.

"Oh, come on. I'm the first person who should know how famous you're going to become. I'm sure it's really good. Can't I just listen to a little bit?" Karen said hopefully.

"Not yet. You'll get a chance to hear it soon," Sarah said and put the CD in her pocket.

When she got home later, she looked through her CD collection in her bedroom. She picked up a Michael Jackson CD. "No one I know listens to this any more," Sarah said to herself. She took the Michael Jackson CD out of its case. Then she put the CD with The Sneakers' song into the case. "No one will ever find it here."

When Justin arrived at home later, he closed the door behind him and ran up to his mum's room. "Mum! We've finished *recording* our song!" Of course Mr Sharp had said that no one should know about the band's project. But Justin knew his mum wouldn't tell anyone. "I'm afraid that I might lose the CD," Justin said to his mother. "Will you keep it in a safe place for me?" His mother said yes and took the CD.

Übung 22: Setze die richtigen Präpositionen ein!
(over, in, into, up, on)

At the same time, Kevin was walking 1. _____ his bedroom. He was looking for a good place to put his copy of 'Secret'. After thinking for a few minutes, he had an idea. He picked 2. _____ the lamp that was 3. _____ a table next to his bed. He put the CD on the table and put the lamp 4. _____ top of the CD. The bottom of the lamp covered the CD perfectly. Kevin wanted to be especially careful. So next, he lit a candle that was 5. _____ his table. He let it burn for a minute. Then he picked it up and held it 6. _____ the bottom of the lamp. He let some wax fall on the bottom of the lamp, where it touched the table. If anyone moved the lamp, the wax would break and Kevin would know that someone had been 7. _____ the room.

Simon also looked around his bedroom for a secret place. But he couldn't find a place that was safe enough.

"I know," he thought. "I'll just bring it with me everywhere that I go." Simon remembered that he always carried his rucksack with him. He opened a small pocket inside his rucksack, put the CD into it and closed it again.

"Now it's safe," he thought. "I will always keep an eye on my rucksack from now on."

Julia shared her bedroom with her younger sister, so she knew she couldn't keep her CD in there. She couldn't find a good place anywhere in her house.

So she put the CD in a plastic bag and went outside. She walked to the centre of her family's garden and made a hole in the ground. She put the plastic-covered CD into the hole and filled the hole up again. Then she used a large stone to mark the place where she had *buried* the CD.

For the rest of the week, the members of The Sneakers were happy and relaxed. Simon celebrated by going back to the CD shop on Wood Street and buying a lot of new albums. He had a lot of fun looking through the different kinds of music and choosing five new CDs.

The only thing he didn't like was the strange man who worked there. Several times he quietly walked up behind Simon – and Simon always jumped when he realized the man was there. And every time Simon turned around to see what the strange man in the leather coat was doing behind him, he asked, "Can I help you?"

Simon also didn't like it when he walked out of the shop and saw Janet. Since the band *auditions*, Simon felt a bit *embarrassed* every time he saw Janet. He was afraid that Janet was still angry with him because he'd been chosen to be the band's singer and guitar player – but Janet hadn't been chosen for anything at all.

Übung 23: Setze das Gegenteil der Wörter in Klammern ein!

However, Janet seemed to be (1. sad) _____.

"*What's up,* Simon? How's the band?" she asked with a very (2. sour) _____ smile.

"Oh, we're okay. I was just shopping for some (3. old) _____ music."

"That's cool. I'm going to meet a friend. See you (4. earlier) _____!" Janet said and walked (5. slowly) _____ into the music shop.

"I guess that Janet has (6. less) _____ self-control than I thought she did. She doesn't seem to be angry about the band at all," Simon thought.

The other band members finally had a chance to do their other hobbies too. Kevin had time to go skateboarding again. Julia was happy that she had time to read and paint again. Justin spent a lot of time playing with his computer. And Sarah spent most of her free time sleeping. She was so tired from the long weeks of rehearsing. Although she normally had so much energy, now she loved being in her bed.

They had worked extremely hard for a long time. But they had sent in their song for the *competition*. Now all they had to do was wait until the winner was chosen. Almost 200 other bands from different parts of England were also taking part in the *competition*. But The Sneakers knew they had made a fantastic song.

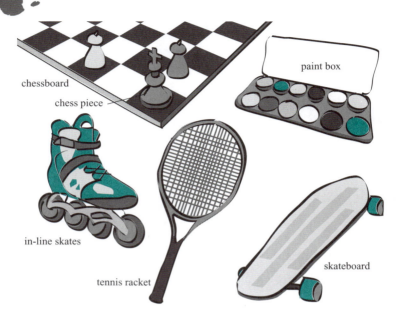

chessboard
chess piece
paint box
in-line skates
tennis racket
skateboard

But some people weren't happy that The Sneakers had such a big secret. A few other kids from school were asking questions about what the five friends were doing. People had some crazy theories about the band's plans. Everybody was very curious about their project.

One boy told people that the group was starting their own record company. Once after school Susie asked Kevin if it was true that the band members were already millionaires.

"No!" Kevin told Susie. "We've only made one song. And we will only get money if we win the …" Kevin stopped talking. He realized he shouldn't be telling Susie so much information.

"Win the what?" Susie asked.

"Uh … nothing, nothing. I have to go," Kevin said quickly and walked away.

Übung 24: Welcher Satz ist die logische Antwort auf die Frage? Kreuze die richtige Lösung an!

1. What would you like to do today?
   a) ☐ I would like a ham sandwich, please.
   b) ☐ I would like to watch a film.
   c) ☐ I would do it if I had time.

2. Where did you buy that dress?
   a) ☐ I bought it in London.
   b) ☐ I bought it on sale.
   c) ☐ I bought it last week.

3. In which direction should we walk?
   a) ☐ We should walk quickly.
   b) ☐ We should walk towards the bank.
   c) ☐ We should walk all day long.

4. What are you thinking about?
   a) ☐ I've been thinking a lot.
   b) ☐ I think so.
   c) ☐ I'm thinking about the CD.

5. Why did you do that?
   a) ☐ I did it, and then I did it again.
   b) ☐ I did it twice.
   c) ☐ I did it because I had to do it.

Sarah's friend, Karen, also wanted to know what was going on. But Sarah didn't tell her anything. At first Karen just made jokes, and tried to make Sarah let her hear the song. But Sarah always said no.

Finally she started becoming angry that Sarah wouldn't share her secret.

"I can't believe you don't tell me things any more," Karen said to Sarah one afternoon.

"You've really changed."

"No I haven't," Sarah said. "I'm not allowed to say anything. I'm really sorry."

But Karen was still angry. "No, you've changed in other ways. You were a punk rocker just a few months ago. Now you're not as wild – not as crazy. I mean, you sleep all the time now. What's happening? I don't know how to say this but … you just seem so silly. And stupid."

Sarah was shocked. "Silly and stupid? You're the one who is getting angry just because you're not allowed to know a little secret. I thought you were my friend. We've known each other for years."

"Well, I WAS your friend," Karen said sarcastically.

"Come on. Don't be like that," Sarah said, trying to be nice. "Let's go to that ska concert tonight. You'll come with me, won't you?"

"Sorry, I've got other plans," Karen said angrily. "And I wouldn't want to keep you awake past your bedtime." She turned around and walked away.

Sarah didn't know what to think. She had been so happy about the band and about their song, 'Secret'. But now her best friend seemed to hate her.

Things continued like this for about two more weeks. Now it was almost the end of the calendar year, close to the winter holidays. The Sneakers were still waiting for the people from the *competition* to choose the winner. Mr Sharp said that they would probably find out the results after the New Year started.

On one especially cold winter day, Justin and Kevin were walking down the corridor at school. Their music lesson had just ended, and they were talking about their plans for the afternoon.

"I'm going to *hang out* with my friend, Joe," Justin said. "Look, there he is."

Kevin looked down the corridor and saw a good-looking boy wearing a big pair of *headphones* walking towards him. But he wasn't just walking – he was dancing too, because he was listening to music. As Joe got closer, Kevin and Justin could see that his *headphones* were *plugged into* a small MP3 player in the pocket of his jeans.

Übung 25: Unterstreiche die neun Wörter, die falsch geschrieben sind, und verbessere sie!

"Hi, Joe," Justin said.
"What?!" Joe shoutid. He took off his *headphones*, and repeeted in a quieter voice, "What? Sorrie, I was just listening to this grate new song."
"I said 'hi'," Justin said. "What song is it? Let me heer."
As Joe gayve the *headphones* to Justin, Justin azked, "Who is the band?"
Joe answered, "I don't know. I've never heard of this band before. All I know is that they rock!"
Justin smild and put the *headphones* over his ears. Suddenly the smile disapeered. His face became as white as snow. His eyes opened wide.
"I told you they were good!" Joe said.
"Wait, something's wrong," Kevin said in a worried voice. "What is it, Justin? You look like you've seen a ghost. Or heard one."

Übung 26: Setze das passende Wort ein!
(song, word, Internet, hands, notes, eyes, day)

Justin couldn't say a 1. _____. Instead, he took off the *headphones* and gave them to Kevin. Kevin only needed to listen to a few 2. _____ of the song playing on Joe's *headphones*. In a second he recognized the notes he had been hearing every 3. _____ for weeks and weeks. He tried to talk: "It's … it's … it's 'Secret'!" He looked at Justin and *whispered*, "It's our 4. _____!"

"What do you mean it's secret?" Joe asked. "The song isn't a secret – I *downloaded* it from the 5. _____."

"Joe!" Justin put his 6. _____ on his friend's shoulders and looked into his 7. _____. "Joe, where exactly did you get this song?"

Joe looked at Justin. The expression on his face showed that he thought Justin was crazy.
"You know that website where you can *download* songs, don't you? It's got a huge collection of songs. I *downloaded* the song from the site's 'New *Releases*' section. Susie told me about it."
"Susie told you? So she knows about the song too?" Justin asked.
"Sure," Joe said. "I was in an Internet chat room last night. Susie and a lot of other kids from school were in there too. And everyone was talking about this song. We all love it!"

Kevin didn't know what to think. One feeling inside him was happiness – because everyone loved the song! But the other feelings were terrible. He was angry. He was *confused*. He had to find out what was happening!

"Uh, Joe, we have to go. See you later," Kevin said quickly. He took Justin's arm and pulled him away from Joe. They started running down the corridor. "We have to tell the others!" Kevin said. He told Justin to go outside and look for anyone who was out there. Then he started looking into every classroom he passed.

"*Oops*, sorry," Kevin said when he opened a classroom door. He had surprised a group of pupils who were taking an exam. He looked inside the boys' toilet and saw Simon looking at himself in the mirror. Simon was *pretending* to play the guitar in the mirror!

"Hey superstar," he said to Simon. "Wake up from your dream. And get ready for your worst *nightmare* to begin!"

Kevin explained what he and Justin had found out.

"It can't be! Someone *released* our song?! We have to find him!" Simon exclaimed.

"Or her," Kevin added.

They left the toilet, and in the corridor they found Justin. Sarah and Julia were standing next to him.

"They both know too," Justin said.

"Okay, Sneakers, let's go to room 363," Kevin said. "Before we do anything else, we have to find Mr Sharp. Maybe he knows what's going on."

Quickly, the band walked to room 363. But when they got there, they found an empty room.

"What?" Sarah shouted in surprise. "Mr Sharp is always here during the day. He stays here until at least three o'clock!" It was noon.

"Forget about Mr Sharp," said Simon. "Whether he's here or not, we have to do something!"

They were all quiet for a few moments. They each tried to think of a good plan.

Übung 27: Finde für das Wort in Klammern ein Reimwort, das in den Zusammenhang passt!

"This is silly," Justin said. "Actually there's nothing to (1. stink) _____ about. The first thing we have to do is (2. mind) _____ our copies of 'Secret'. If one of the five CDs is missing, then we know who (3. cost) _____ it. And then we can start to find out who (4. look) _____ it – and why."

The rest of the (5. hand) _____ members agreed. Before the band left the classroom, Simon slowly opened his rucksack. He didn't want his (6. ends) _____ to see him looking for his copy of the CD. What if it wasn't there? What if HE lost the CD? He had to make (7. cure) _____ that it was there without anyone noticing.

"Hey, Simon! What are you doing?" Sarah had seen Simon opening his rucksack. He had a strange expression on his face, and she wanted to know why.
"Oh, um, nothing. Just looking for … something," he answered.
Sarah looked at Simon, and her eyes grew big with shock. "Oh, no. Don't tell me that you kept your CD in your rucksack. Pleeeeeease don't tell me you are such a huge idiot!"

"Well," Simon answered nervously, "I always have my rucksack with me. I thought nothing could happen to the CD."

Sarah picked up Simon's rucksack and let everything in it fall onto the floor. The CD wasn't there. She looked inside the rucksack. She opened the little pocket where Simon had put the CD.

"Empty," she said.

"Oh, no," he said. "I thought …"

"You thought wrong!" said Kevin. He sounded angry.

"Hey wait," Simon said. "Maybe it fell out in my room."

"We'll see," Justin said. Everyone seemed to be angry with Simon. Then The Sneakers left room 363. After school, they all went to find their copies of the band's song.

When Justin got home, he looked for his mum in every room of the house. But he couldn't find her anywhere.

"She must be at work," he thought. So he went to the living room and found her telephone number at work. His mum always told him that he should use that number only if there was an *emergency*.

"If this isn't an *emergency*, I don't know what is," Justin said to himself as he picked up the phone.

"Hello?" said his mum's voice.

"Mum! I'm so glad you're there!"

"Is that you, Justin?" she asked. She sounded worried. "What's wrong? What is it?"

"Mum, where's that CD I gave you? I need it – NOW!"

His mother laughed. "Is that the problem? Oh, I was so afraid. I thought it was something serious."

"It is serious!" said Justin.

"Okay, fine. Sorry. Let me think – where did I put it?" She was quiet for a moment. "Oh, yes! I put it in the oven!"

"The OVEN? Are you crazy? I asked you to keep it safe!"

"That's the safest place I knew. I never make cakes or biscuits. I never use the oven for anything. It's the only place in the house where no one ever looks."

Übung 28: *Welche Gegenteile gehören zusammen? Trage die richtige Nummer in das Kästchen ein!*

1. safe
2. empty
3. rich
4. excited
5. back
6. often

☐ full
☐ calm
☐ front
☐ seldom
☐ dangerous
☐ poor

"Thanks mum!" Justin said quickly and put down the phone. He ran to the kitchen and opened the oven. The CD wasn't there!

However, the oven wasn't empty. There was something silver at the bottom of the oven. Justin realized that the oven smelled terrible. It smelled like … burnt plastic. He suddenly understood that the silver *stuff* in the oven was his CD. But it was completely *melted*.

"There you are!" Justin heard the voice of his older sister, Anne. "Was it you who put that stupid CD in there? That's an oven, you idiot. It's not a CD player!"

"What did you do to it?" Justin asked.

"I had to make biscuits for my cookery class. It was a homework project. I started mixing things together to make the biscuits. Then I turned on the oven to heat it up. But when I opened the oven to put the biscuits inside, a huge cloud of smoke came out," Anne explained. "Now what do I do about my project?"

Justin was too excited to answer his sister.

"Should I be sad or happy?" he asked himself. His copy of the song had been destroyed. That was terrible. But at least he could tell the others that it wasn't his fault that the CD was on the Internet now.

As Justin started cleaning the *melted* plastic from his mum's oven, Sarah was looking for Michael Jackson. She was sitting on the floor of her bedroom. All around her was chaos. There were CDs all over the floor. Some of the cases were opened. She had looked through her whole collection of CDs. But she couldn't find the CD case with the photo of Michael Jackson on it – the CD case with 'Secret' inside. Suddenly Sarah lost all her energy. She felt so tired. So she lay down in the middle of her CDs and fell asleep.

When she woke up, she saw her dad's shoes in front of her face. She looked up and saw her dad looking down at her, smiling. How long had she slept? Thirty minutes? An hour? Longer?

"I see you're tidying up your room," Sarah's dad said with a bit of sarcasm. "So, you're starting by organizing your CDs?" He laughed.

"What are you laughing about?" Sarah asked sadly.

"What's wrong? Oh – I know. You're probably sad about the *fight* you had with Karen."

"How did you know about that?" Sarah was shocked. She hadn't told her dad about her *fight* with her best friend.

"Karen told me," her dad explained.

"Karen? When did you talk to Karen?"

"Didn't I tell you? She came here yesterday evening," he said. "You were out, at that ska concert. She came here around eight o'clock. She said something about a *fight* that you two had. She told me that she didn't want to be your friend any more. And she said that she wanted to take some of her things back. I've known Karen as long as you have – almost seven years. I didn't really think she was serious about the *fight*. So I let her go into your room."

"You did what?!" Sarah shouted.

Her dad was surprised. "What's the problem? She only took her dirty old denim jacket and two CDs."

"She didn't take a Michael Jackson CD, did she?"

"Yes, she did."

Sarah sat down in a chair and covered her face with her hands.

"What? I thought you hated Michael Jackson now. Let her have that old CD. Why is it so important to you?"

*Übung 29: Vervollständige die Sätze mit **anything, nothing, anybody** oder **nobody**!*

1. The band can't tell their plans to _____!

2. _____ wants to come to the cinema with me.

3. I don't want _____ to eat. I'm not hungry.

4. Sarah's not afraid of _____.

5. There's _____ interesting happening right now.

Sarah pushed her hands up to the top of her head and started pulling her short, pink hair. "Dad, you don't understand! That wasn't just a Michael Jackson CD. It wasn't a Michael Jackson CD at all. It was … Oh, forget it."

Sarah couldn't continue speaking. Could it be true? Had her best friend stolen their song? Had Karen put the song on the Internet to destroy the band's chances of winning the *competition*? Did she want *to get her revenge* because Sarah had been spending so much time with the band? It was all too much for Sarah to understand. She and Karen had been friends for almost seven years. Karen wouldn't destroy seven years of friendship because of one little *fight* – would she? Sarah simply didn't want to believe that Karen had done something so bad.

"Maybe it wasn't Karen at all," she thought. "Maybe it was Justin! He wasn't in our music class until he got into the band. Then he asked to transfer into the class. He's an outsider. What do we really know about Justin? All I know about him is that he loves computers. It was probably simple for him to put the song on the Internet. It's him! Tomorrow I'll tell the others that Justin must be behind all of this. It wasn't Karen."

Kevin was worried as he opened the door to his room. His bedroom was on the ground floor of his family's house. And he had a big window that was never *locked*. Kevin's family lived in a safe area, and he never thought that he had to *lock* his window. But maybe a thief had entered his room through the window. Maybe someone had found the secret place where he had put his copy of 'Secret'.

When he walked to the table with the special lamp on it, he saw that everything looked the same. He looked for the place where he had put the *melted* wax. The wax was not broken. He could see a bit of silver under the lamp. The CD was still there! Kevin picked up the lamp. The wax broke into many small pieces. That meant that no one had looked under the lamp since he put the CD there.

"Well, now we know that the thief didn't steal MY copy of the song," he thought.

Later that evening, Julia finally arrived home. While Justin, Sarah and Kevin were looking for their CDs, Julia had been sitting in a chair at the dentist's. She had asked her parents to let her miss the *appointment*. But they said no. So Julia had to spend most of the afternoon waiting to have her teeth checked by the dentist. As the dentist checked her teeth for holes, Julia was thinking about the hole in her family's garden. Was the CD still *buried* in the hole?

When Julia got home it was already quite dark outside. As soon as she got out of her parents' car, she ran behind the house to the garden. There was some snow on the ground, and she almost fell as she ran. Julia was just a few steps away from the place where she had *buried* the CD. But she could see that something was different. The snow on the ground was white with the light of the moon. But in the middle of the garden, the ground was dark. She stepped closer.

"Ouch!" Julia shouted. She had hit her toe on something hard. She looked down and saw the large stone that she had used to mark the special place in the garden. But someone had moved it.

> **Übung 30:** *Unterstreiche im folgenden Textabschnitt die Synonyme für die Wörter in Klammern!*
> ***(1. found 2. place 3. created 4. part 5. perfect 6. path)***

Julia got down on her hands and knees. Someone had discovered the location where the CD was! Someone had made a hole in the ground. Julia started moving the earth away with her hands. But the only thing she found was a piece of the plastic bag that the CD had been in.

"This was the ideal place!" Julia said to herself. "Who could have known that the CD was here?"

She looked around to see if she could find any *clues*. Soon she noticed something in the snow. There was very little light, so it was hard for Julia to see. But she thought she saw some marks in the snow. They made a *trail* that started at the hole in the middle of the garden. She followed the *trail* with her eyes and saw that they went to the garden behind the next house.

Julia stood up and walked towards the next house. She saw that the *trail* of marks went through the next garden. They ended at the back door of her *neighbour*'s house. The family who lived in that house were the Sands. There was Mr Sand, Mrs Sand – and their daughter, Susie Sand.

Susie Sand? That was the girl who had flirted with Kevin a few weeks ago. But Julia remembered something more important than that. Susie was the girl who had *auditioned* to be the band's keyboard player – but Mr Sharp hadn't chosen her.

"Why wasn't I more careful?" Julia asked herself. "Maybe Susie wanted to stop the band from winning the *competition*, because she isn't in the band. Maybe she saw me put the CD in my garden the other day. She probably knew what I was doing. And then she took the CD out of the hole and put the song on the Internet!"

Julia was shocked. Should she knock on Susie's door? No – she had to tell the others! Together they would make a plan. Suddenly Julia realized that she was very cold. And her hands were covered with dirt. She started walking back to her house.

"Aaaah!" Julia shouted. A loud noise had surprised her. She covered her mouth with her hands and looked around. What had made that noise? Was Susie watching her? She looked back at the Sands' house and saw the face of their pet dog, Hunter, in one of the windows. The dog was *barking*. Julia hoped that Hunter's *barking* hadn't made anyone notice that she was outside. She quickly went back inside her house.

The next day The Sneakers all arrived at school early so that they could tell Mr Sharp everything that had happened. They entered room 363 and saw their teacher sitting at his desk.

"Mr Sharp!" they all shouted at the same time. "Someone stole our song and put in on the Internet!"

Übung 31: Schreibe die Zahlen aus!

1. 32 _____

2. 1ˢᵗ _____

3. 13ᵗʰ _____

4. $^1/_2$ _____

5. 8,300 _____

6. 502 _____

Justin continued explaining, "A lot of kids here at school have MP3 copies of it! What are we going to do? There's no chance that we can win the national *competition* now!"

Mr Sharp became very serious. "This is terrible. How could anyone do this?" he said. He thought for a moment. "Okay, *guys* – we can't talk about this here. We have to find a safer place to discuss this. Everyone meet me after school. We'll meet at the café in the town centre. They have a table at the back that's quiet and private."

The Sneakers agreed.

At the end of the school day, the band members met outside the school and started walking to the café. It was a sunny day and the snow on the ground was starting to *melt*.

"Where's Simon?" Kevin asked.

The others looked around. Kevin was right. Simon wasn't there.

"Well, he knows where we're meeting," Sarah said. "He's probably waiting for us at the café."

But when they arrived at the café, Simon wasn't there. But Mr Sharp was. Their teacher was sitting at the back of the café, at a table in a dark corner. He was drinking a big cup of black coffee. Julia ordered a tea, and everyone else ordered hot chocolate. The waitress was walking away when Simon ran into the café saying, "I'd like cup of coffee, please!" Then he sat down and explained why he was late.

"I've been looking everywhere, *guys*," Simon said quickly. "I'm so sorry, but it seems that everything is my fault. I couldn't find the CD anywhere. I've looked in every room in my house. I've wandered through the streets. I've looked everywhere! I'm sorry. I understand if you all hate me now."

"Slow down, Simon," Julia said. "You're not the only person who can't find their CD. Mine is gone too."

"At least mine is okay," Kevin said.

"Mine is *melted*," Justin said.

Sarah looked at Justin angrily. "That's not true," Sarah said. "I think you're the one who put our song on the Internet." She looked at Kevin, Simon, Julia and Mr Sharp. "Listen, Justin isn't from our original music class. He's a computer *freak*. Here is my theory – he hates us for some reason and decided to make it impossible for us to win the *competition*. Maybe he's angry because we weren't friends with him until he joined the band. I don't really know why Justin did it – but he did!"

The others were shocked. Especially Justin, who almost looked like he was going to cry.

"I … I tell you I didn't do it!" he said. "Why would I do something like that? I want to win the *competition* as much as anyone else!"

"Well, you ARE the computer expert, Justin," Simon said.

"You're just saying that because you're afraid that it's all your fault!" Justin said. "You lost your CD so now you're agreeing with Sarah. It's so easy to say that the new *guy* did it!" Then he explained how his CD had *melted*.

Übung 32: Trage die fehlenden Buchstaben des beschriebenen Adjektivs in die Lücken ein!

1. no longer alive	_ e _ d
2. having a lot of power	_ tr _ _ g
3. regular or standard	n _ _ m _ _
4. not dirty	_ l _ a _
5. inexpensive	_ _ e _ p
6. prepared	r _ _ _ y

Julia *interrupted* the *argument*. "Wait a minute, Sarah. What happened to your CD? Maybe YOU put the song on the Internet."

"That's impossible," Sarah said.

"Why?"

"Because … I can't tell you."

"That's a good explanation," Justin said sarcastically.

Sarah looked angry. But then her expression changed to one of sadness. "Oh no!" she said. "I can't believe what I've been saying. Justin, I'm sorry." Sarah told them about her *fight* with her best friend, Karen. She explained what had happened the night before. She said that she thought Karen had taken her copy of 'Secret'.

"I just can't believe that Karen would do something like this. She is – or was – my best friend. So instead of telling you all the truth, I decided to say that Justin did it. Justin, can you forgive me?"

"I understand, Sarah," Justin answered. "But we have to stop being angry with each other."

"Justin is right," said Julia. "We all wanted to win this *competition*. So there's no reason why any of us would want to destroy our chances. We're all in this together." Then she explained what she had found in her garden the night before. She said that she had found a *trail* in the snow that led to Susie Sand's house.

Kevin *frowned*. "No, Susie wouldn't do something like that," he said. "She's so sweet."

"You're only saying that because she flirted with you," Simon said. "Girls can do some very strange things. One minute they're nice to you. And the next minute they steal the thing that's most important to you – and destroy your career."

"Simon is being a bit dramatic," Justin said. "It's not fair to say it's anyone's fault until we find out what really happened. But he's right – we can't trust anyone any more."

"At least we have each other," Julia said.

Mr Sharp had been listening quietly and drinking his coffee. But he had also seemed to be thinking about something else. When The

Sneakers finished talking he said, "So, let me see if I understand. One copy has been destroyed. And three copies are missing. Is that right?"

The others said yes.

"But that's not all we have to worry about," he said. "I've been thinking. There were five copies of the song. But there was also the master copy – the copy I sent to the *competition*." He was quiet for a moment. Then he continued, "All of this might really be my fault. Do you remember the day we *recorded* the song? After you all left the studio, I stayed for a while. I worked on the song because I wanted to make it absolutely perfect. When I left the studio I was quite tired. And I left the CD in the studio overnight."

"*So what*?" said Kevin. "It's your studio. You're allowed to leave things there, aren't you?"

"Yes, it's my studio. But don't forget that my business partner, Al, works there too," Mr Sharp said. "Al is a good *guy*. But he has changed a bit over the years. At the beginning he *cared about* music and about art. But now all he seems to *care about* is money. Maybe he wanted to make some extra money by putting your song on the Internet. And I also forgot to tell him the special rule for the *competition* – the rule that says the song must be brand new and can't be *released* before the *competition*."

"Oh no!" said The Sneakers.

"What should we do now?" Justin asked.

Julia answered, "We have to start finding out what really happened. I'll try to find out if Susie is the thief."

"I know that no one took my copy of the song," said Kevin. "So I'll help you, Julia."

"And I'll help you, Sarah," Justin said. "You and I will find out if Karen stole the song *to get her revenge*."

"But Karen didn't … she couldn't have …" Sarah stuttered.

"But she might have," said Justin. "We have to *investigate* every *clue*."
"What should I do?" Simon asked. "I've looked everywhere for my CD, but I can't find it. I don't know where else I should look."
"You can come with me, Simon," said Mr Sharp. "Together we can find out if Al is behind all this. And I'll also *contact* the people who own the website where the song is now. Maybe they can tell me the name of the person who put it there." Then he turned to the others and said, "Okay, everyone, you all know what you have to do. So let's go!"

Übung 33: Setze die Verben in der richtigen Zeitform ein!

Mr Sharp and The Sneakers (1. to pay) _____ for their drinks and (2. to leave) _____ the café. Julia and Kevin walked away in one direction. Sarah and Justin walked in the opposite direction. And Simon and Mr Sharp (3. to get) _____ into Mr Sharp's white van and (4. to drive) _____ away.

Julia and Kevin walked quietly for a while. Finally, Kevin asked Julia, "Where are we (5. to go) _____ now?"

"We're going to my house. I'll (6. to show) _____ you where I had *buried* the CD. And then we'll find out the facts about sweet little Susie," Julia (7. to explain) _____.

A little while later Julia and Kevin arrived at Julia's house.
"Come with me. The garden is behind the house," Julia said.

When they reached the garden, Julia noticed that there was no longer any snow on the ground. The sun had *melted* it all.

"So here's the hole," Kevin said. "But I don't see any *footprints* in the snow. There's no *trail* going between the hole and Susie's house. I told you that Susie had nothing to do with it."

"It was here last night!" Julia said. "I saw the marks in the moonlight. I'm sure Susie had something to do with it."

"I'm not," said Kevin. "She's a cool girl. Yes, it's true that she didn't get chosen to be the band's keyboard player. But she's too nice to do something so heartless."

"Come on, Kevin. You're in love with that girl. Naturally you think she's 'cool' and 'nice'. But we have to see things clearly. We have to get more information."

"And how do you think we should do that?" Kevin asked.

"We have to go inside Susie's house," Julia answered.

"What?! You mean you want us to break into her house?!"

"WE aren't going to do anything. YOU are going to get into her house. But you won't have to break in. If Susie is really behind this, she won't want us to realize that anything is wrong. And she won't stop flirting with you. So all you have to do is go to her house and ask her to invite you in!" Julia said.

"I can't do that," Kevin said. "You want me to ask her to let me in – and then you want me to look around her house for clues? I'm a terrible actor! She will know I'm not serious."

"But you are serious," said Julia. "You are serious about liking her, aren't you? You're attracted to her. Just be natural. You'll be fine."

Julia and Kevin argued for a few more minutes. Finally Kevin realized that this was their only chance to find out if Susie had anything to do with the missing CD. And because Kevin wanted to show that Susie was *innocent*, he agreed to try the plan. So he combed his hair and tried to look as nice as he could. Then he walked over to Susie's front door and knocked three times. Several seconds later the door opened. First Kevin saw Susie's curly black hair. Then he looked down at her face.

"Hi Kevin. What are you doing here?"

"Um, hi, Susie. I was just skateboarding along the street and I saw your bicycle outside this house. I thought it must be where you live, so I decided to knock on your door and say hi," Kevin said.

Susie looked down at Kevin's hands. They were empty. "Where's your skateboard?" she asked.

"My skateboard?" Kevin said nervously. "Oh … I … left it in a bush. It's a bit dirty and I didn't want to get any earth on the grass outside your house."

"You didn't want to get any earth on the grass? The grass grows in earth!" But Susie started smiling. "You're so silly Kevin. But I like that. Silly boys are sweet."

Übung 34: In diesem Gitternetz sind vier Pflanzenarten versteckt. Findest du sie alle?

A	M	G	T
L	E	R	R
N	K	A	E
R	O	S	E
B	U	S	H

_____

_____

_____

_____

Kevin's face turned red. He was getting more and more nervous. But he had to remember the plan.

"So, Susie, I wanted to know if you have some free time now. I think it's a pity that you weren't chosen to be in the band with me. But I wanted to know if you would play a song for me on your keyboard. I've never heard you play."

Susie was *thrilled*. "Of course! Come in!" She led Kevin into her house. After he was inside, he took off his coat. As he was hanging it up, he looked down and saw a big, black dog come running towards him. The dog jumped up and *licked* Kevin's face.

"Oh, that's *disgusting*!" Kevin said. The dog started biting Kevin's trousers and his shoes.

"Don't worry about Hunter," Susie said. "He jumps onto every new person. He likes to bite clothes, but he won't bite you. He likes to chew on anything he can find. Stop Hunter! Go!"

The dog let go of Kevin's trousers and went away.

"Let's go up to my bedroom. My keyboard is in there."

Susie and Kevin went up the stairs to Susie's bedroom. Her room had light-blue walls and a large bed. There was a white desk in the corner. In the middle of the room was a black chair and an electric keyboard. Susie led Kevin to the bed and told him to sit down.

"I'll be right back," she said and left the room. Kevin heard her walk into the bathroom and close the door. Quickly he jumped up from the bed and started looking around the room. First he looked through Susie's CD collection. There was a lot of pop music, a few hip-hop albums – but no copy of 'Secret'. Then he opened the drawers in the desk. Pencils, pens, paper, some old letters – but *no* CD here *either*. Where else should he look? Under the bed! Nothing.

He was looking through Susie's bookshelves when he heard the bathroom door open. He didn't have time to run back to the bed. So he just stood there, ready to tell Susie the truth. But when Susie saw Kevin standing in front of her bookshelves, she didn't get angry. She was happy!

"Oh, Kevin! You're so sweet! You're trying to find out what kind of books I like!" she said in a happy voice. "You really do *care about* me, don't you?"

"Um, sure, I think you're a nice girl," Kevin said. He wasn't lying. He wasn't really in love with Susie – but he did find her attractive. She had a pretty face and lovely blue eyes. "Of course she likes me," he thought. "I'm in a rock band and I'm almost famous."

Susie took Kevin back to the bed. He sat down and she sat down next to him.

"Aren't you going to play a song for me?" Kevin asked.

"I'd prefer to do something else," Susie said. She moved closer to Kevin. Her clear, blue eyes were looking into Kevin's green eyes. A little voice inside Kevin's head said, "*What about* the plan? The CD!" But the little voice disappeared when Susie's lips touched his.

Übung 35: Unterstreiche die fünf Sätze, die inhaltlich nicht zum Text passen!

At the same time that Susie opened her front door, Simon and Mr Sharp arrived at the building with the sign for 'Sam's Studios' on it. "Does that mean your first name is Sam, Mr Sharp?" Simon asked while *pointing to* the sign. Then his mum turned the television off.

"That's right, Simon," Mr Sharp answered. "Come on, let's go inside. I think it's some kind of cat."

It was a weekday afternoon, so Mr Sharp thought his partner, Al, would be in the studios. The bank isn't open on Sundays. But when he reached the door, he found that it was *locked*.

"Hmm, that's strange," Mr Sharp said. Justin wanted to go home. He took out his keys and unlocked the door. The whole building was quiet. There was a party happening. When they entered the recording room they saw that it was empty.

"That's strange," Mr Sharp said. "I thought he would be working with one of his bands today. Maybe he's in the office." He led Simon to a door on the right side of the room. The door was unlocked and they went inside.

The office was filled with papers and CDs. It looked completely unorganized and Simon wondered how they would ever find any *clues* in all the chaos.

"Al isn't very good at keeping things neat," Mr Sharp said. He went to the desk and picked up a cup of coffee. "It's still warm, Al must have gone a few minutes ago. It looks like we have a little time to look around." Simon started looking through the CDs that were in short *stacks* around the room. Maybe he would find a copy of 'Secret'. Mr Sharp looked though the papers on Al's desk.

"All I see here are a lot of *bills*," Mr Sharp said.

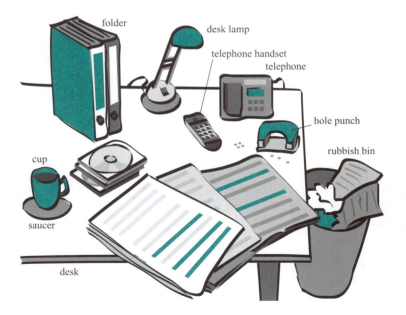

After about ten minutes, Simon started to get worried. "Maybe we should go, Mr Sharp."

"You're right, Simon," Mr Sharp said. "It seems that Al had nothing to do with this."

They started to leave the room. But as Simon turned around, he saw a piece of paper hanging out of the *rubbish bin*. Was he crazy? Did he really see the letters S-N-E-A-K on the paper? He picked it up. No, he wasn't crazy – on the piece of paper was a drawing of a big running shoe. And above the shoe was written 'The Sneakers'.

"Look, Mr Sharp! What does this mean?"

"I'm not sure, Simon," Mr Sharp answered. "It looks like a design for a CD *cover*. Could it be that Al wants to start selling The Sneakers' song? I can't believe it! I mean, I know that Al has become more and more interested in money. But I can't believe he would do this. Al and I have been friends since I was at university. I can't believe he could be a *backstabber*! However, Al does have a lot of *bills* here in his office. Maybe he needs some extra money. But we can talk about that later. Let's get out of here."

Simon took the drawing and followed Mr Sharp out of the building.

Übung 36: Welche Übersetzung der kursiv markierten Slang-Ausdrücke stimmt? Kreuze die richtige Lösung an!

1. *What the heck* are you doing?
   a) ☐ Was zum Teufel machst du?
   b) ☐ Was ist los?

2. This band is totally *wicked*!
   a) ☐ Diese Band ist total furchtbar!
   b) ☐ Diese Band ist total geil!

3. She's a really cool *chick*.
   a) ☐ Sie ist echt ein tolles Mädel.
   b) ☐ Sie ist echt eine tolle Schauspielerin.

4. I'm completely *knackered*!
   a) ☐ Ich bin total besoffen!
   b) ☐ Ich bin total müde!

5. I heard that he *nicked* a CD and got into trouble.
   a) ☐ Ich habe gehört, dass er eine CD gekauft hat und in Schwierigkeiten geraten ist.
   b) ☐ Ich habe gehört, dass er eine CD geklaut hat und in Schwierigkeiten geraten ist.

While all this was happening, Sarah and Justin were trying to think of a way to *investigate* the role Karen might have played in all this. They were sitting in Justin's living room.

"There's no way to get into Karen's bedroom," Sarah said.

"She doesn't even let her parents go into her room. She keeps a huge lock on the door. And she keeps the key on a *necklace* that she always wears."

"But how can we find out any information, Sarah?" Justin asked. "We have to find out what she did with that CD!"

Sarah started thinking and was quiet for several minutes. Finally, she said, "I have an idea. Let's get our bikes. We're going to the *local indoor swimming pool*."

As they were riding their bikes down the street, Sarah explained that Karen was on the school's swimming team. Most evenings of the week she trained with the team between five o'clock and half past six.

"If we go there now, maybe we'll find her *locker*," Sarah continued.

"Karen takes her laptop computer with her almost everywhere she goes. If we can get her computer, you can find out if she's the person who put our song on the Internet."

"Me?!" Justin said in surprise.

"Of course you," said Sarah. "You're the computer expert. You know everything about the Internet and websites. You should be able to check her *files* and see if she's put any *files* on the Internet. Can you do that?"

"Well …," Justin began nervously. "I know how to do it. But should we do it?"

"It's our only choice, Justin. Look, we're at the pool," Sarah said. They got off their bikes and walked into the building. They passed one door and smelled *chlorine* in the air and heard the sounds of water. Then they reached a door with 'Ladies' written on it.

"Let's go," Sarah said and opened the door.

"That's the ladies' *changing room*. I can't go in there!" Justin said.

"Nobody is in there. Everyone is in the pool training now, and they'll stay there for another hour. Now let's go!" Sarah said.

Justin didn't like this plan. But he followed Sarah into the ladies' *changing room*. They walked past rows of closed *lockers*. In front of each *locker* was a pair of shoes. Finally Sarah stopped and said, "There!" She walked to a pair of black *trainers* with white stars painted on them. Then she looked up at the *locker*. There was a big, pink *combination lock* on it.

"Oh no! Now what?" Justin asked.

"What would her combination be? Let me think," Sarah said. A few moments later she said, "I know!"

Justin watched as she turned the *combination lock* to the numbers 29 – 12 – 83. The lock opened!

"I knew it! She's totally in love with the lead singer from an American band called The Stints, and 29 December 1983 is his birthday."

Übung 37: *Finde für die britischen Begriffe auf der linken Seite das amerikanische Gegenstück! Trage die richtige Nummer in das Kästchen ein!*

1. flat
2. holiday
3. lorry
4. lift
5. *trainer*
6. rubbish

☐ elevator
☐ garbage
☐ apartment
☐ *sneaker*
☐ truck
☐ vacation

Sarah put her hand into Karen's *locker* and pulled out a black bag. She opened the bag and pulled out a laptop computer. "Come on, let's go somewhere where no one will see you," Sarah said.

"I thought you said everyone was in the pool."

"They are. But we have to be safe. Here, you can sit on the toilet and close the door of the *cubicle*," Sarah said. Justin got inside and Sarah closed the door. "Pick up your feet!" Sarah said. "Good. I'll be right back."

"Sarah, where are you going?!" Justin asked with a worried voice. But Sarah had already left. Justin decided to try to relax and start working. He worked on the computer for about twenty minutes when he heard a door open and two girls laughing.

"Wait a second," one girl's voice said. "I've got to go to the *loo*."

Justin stopped breathing. What would he do if a girl found him sitting on a toilet in the ladies'? The *cubicle* door moved. Someone was trying to open it.

"Is someone in there?" the voice asked.

Justin was screaming on the inside. He didn't know what to do. He would get into very serious trouble if someone found him with Karen's computer – in the girls' *loo*! But instead of screaming, he answered in a high voice, doing his best imitation of a girl, "Just a minute."

For a moment Justin heard nothing. Did the girls outside know that they were hearing the voice of a boy?

Finally the girl's voice said, "Come on, Liz, let's use the *loo* in the corridor." He heard them walking away and continued working on Karen's computer. A little while later Sarah came back and asked if Justin was okay.

"You're lucky that I'm okay! I almost got *caught*!" he said angrily. Then he opened the door of the toilet *cubicle* and said, "I've finished."

Sarah looked excited and worried at the same time. She wanted to know if Karen was the person who put 'Secret' on the Internet. But she was also afraid to find out her best friend did something so bad. She closed her eyes and asked, "So, was it Karen?"

"I've looked through all her Internet *files*," Justin said. "I can see that she *downloaded* the song from a website. However, I can't find anything that shows that she put the song on the website. She only *downloaded* the song as an MP3."

"So does that mean she's *innocent*?" Sarah asked.

"Well, it's possible that she gave the CD to someone else – and that person put the song on the Internet. But one thing is sure: Karen didn't do it herself."

Übung 38: Beantworte die Fragen zum Text!

1. Why does Mr Sharp think Al needs money?

2. Where did Justin and Sarah find Karen's computer?

3. Where did Justin hide in the ladies' *changing room?*

_____

4. Who almost found Justin where he was hiding?

_____

5. Did Karen put The Sneakers' song on the Internet?

_____

Sarah smiled. Of course Karen hadn't done it! Sarah felt so much better now that she knew that Karen was *innocent*.
She and Justin put the computer back into the bag in Karen's *locker*. Then they replaced the *combination lock* and left the building.
As soon as they walked outside into the cold winter air, Justin felt much better. He didn't like *sneaking* around like that. And he had never been in the ladies' *changing room* before – what an adventure! Sarah also felt better. She finally knew for sure that Karen hadn't wanted *to get her revenge* on her.
"Now what?" Justin asked as he got on his bike.
"Now nothing," Sarah answered. "We've done everything we could do. When we see the others tomorrow morning, we'll tell them what we've found out. And I'll have to talk to Karen soon. I have to get that CD back to make sure that it doesn't fall into the wrong hands. See you tomorrow, Justin."
"Okay, see you then. Bye!"
Justin and Sarah rode away into the darkness.

At about the same time, Julia saw Kevin walk out of Susie Sand's house. Julia had been sitting in the living room of her house for more than an hour. Through the living room window she could see the front door of Susie's house. She had been sitting on the sofa, drinking from a bottle of Coke, waiting nervously for Kevin. Several times she'd asked herself why Kevin was staying in there so long. Did Susie know why he was there? He should have finished searching for the CD after about fifteen minutes, Julia thought.

When she looked out the window and finally saw his head covered with *shaggy* brown hair, she jumped up from the sofa and ran to her own front door. Normally Julia was quiet and relaxed – but now she felt like she was going crazy. When Kevin reached Julia's door, she looked at him with wild eyes.

"So? What, what, what? Was it her? Did Susie want to hurt the band because she wasn't chosen to be in it? Come on, tell me!" Julia said.

"What? Susie wouldn't hurt a fly," Kevin said.

Julia noticed that his voice sounded strange. And what was that strange light in his eyes? And what was that on his cheek? Was he bleeding? Had Susie hit him? Julia moved closer to Kevin and looked at his cheek. Lipstick?!

Übung 39: Wähle das passende Wort für jeden Satz aus und unterstreiche es!

1. They must find out witch/which person stole their song.
2. That's the place where/were they first met.
3. I don't know if its/it's such a good idea.
4. Julia waited four/for a very long time.
5. Julia was very surprising/surprised when she saw Kevin.
6. She didn't want to put him in danger/dangerous.

"*What the heck* were you doing over there?" Julia shouted. Kevin didn't seem to react.

"We have to be detectives, Kevin! Objective detectives," Julia said. "We have to look for *clues* and find out who stole our song – remember? Or did you forget that someone stole our song and put it on the Internet – and probably destroyed our chances of winning FIVE THOUSAND pounds?!"

"You don't understand, Julia. Susie had nothing to do with it," he said.

"How do you know that? Did you even look for the CD while you were in there? Or did you two just *snog* the whole time?" Julia asked. There was anger and shock in her voice.

"Well, um … I did look in her room," Kevin said defensively. "But I couldn't find the CD anywhere. I started looking through the things on her bookshelves when she came back into the room. And after that … well … I stopped looking."

Julia couldn't believe what she was hearing.

"So you looked around her bedroom for, what, five minutes? And then what? Did you play cards? Did you help her with her homework?" Julia asked sarcastically.

Kevin's face turned red. He finally realized what he had really done. How could he tell the others what had happened? Would he tell them that he couldn't look for *clues* because he was too busy falling in love? But he really was in love! Kevin couldn't understand why he hadn't noticed Susie earlier. There had been a time when he liked other girls – Janet, for example. But he'd never spoken to Susie before the day of the band *auditions*.

Übung 40: Welches Wort ist das „schwarze Schaf"?

1. juice, Coke, lemon, water
2. taste, chew, *lick*, smell
3. butter, bitter, sour, sweet

4. cup, plate, glass, oven
5. sausage, egg, beef, ham
6. eat, bake, roast, fry
7. cut, open, slice, chop

"Julia, something wonderful has happened," Kevin started to explain. "I think I've fallen in love."
Julia was so shocked that she couldn't speak for a few moments. Finally, her sweet, sentimental side broke through her shock.
"That's really great, Kevin," she said with a smile. But then, more seriously, "But maybe she's just *pretending* to like you so that you won't think she put our song on the Internet. Maybe she's just acting. We need to find out what happened to our song. Susie's got a copy of it, I know it. We have to find out why – and what she's done with it."
They were both quiet for a minute. Kevin was quiet because he felt bad about *letting his friends down*. Julia was quiet because she was trying to think of a new plan.
"It seems that you're going to be pretty useless for finding out information about Susie," Julia began. "Well, you might be able to find out whether she's a good kisser or not – but not whether she's a thief or not. So I'll have to do things myself."
"What's your plan?" Kevin asked.
"It's too late for me to go over there now. I'll have to try it tomorrow afternoon, after school. But I probably shouldn't tell you more. Maybe you'll see Susie again tonight and tell your new love everything."
"Hey, that's not fair," Kevin said. But he didn't keep arguing because he knew he had *messed up* their original plan.
"Okay, I'll see you tomorrow morning at school," Kevin said sadly as he left Julia's house.

"Yeah. See you then," Julia said and closed the door behind him.
The next day The Sneakers met during the lunch break to discuss the results of their *investigations*. Sarah and Justin went first.
"We don't have to worry about Karen any more. We know for sure that she didn't put 'Secret' on the Internet," Sarah explained.
"How do you know that? Why are you so sure?" Simon asked.
Sarah and Justin looked at each other, but didn't answer the question. They didn't really want to tell the others how they had found out their information. They both knew that what they did was very risky – and a bit wrong too.
After several moments of nervous silence, Sarah and Justin started explaining what they had done. They made clear that they knew they had put themselves in danger. And they knew it was bad to take something that belongs to someone else – even if you're doing it to prove that the person is *innocent*.

Übung 41: Setze die richtigen Präpositionen ein! *(of, out, on, in, away, up)*

1. No one wants to give _____ any information.

2. Maybe Sarah will let her short hair grow _____.

3. If The Sneakers win the *competition*, they could go _____ tour.

4. Will all this make Karen and Sarah split _____ as friends?

5. All the band members have a lot _____ stories to tell the others.

6. The teenagers explained what happened _____ their *investigations*.

"But you have to understand," Sarah said. "This band means so much to us. We'd do anything to find out who did this terrible thing to us. Karen is my best friend. It broke my heart to think that she might have done this to me. And I feel terrible now that I know she really had nothing to do with it. But I had to find out. I had to!"

"Maybe we shouldn't tell Mr Sharp what we've done," Justin said. "He might be really angry that we didn't tell him about our plan before we did it. But although it was bad, we were ready to do anything to find out the truth. We're sorry that it had to be this way. But at least we have one *suspect* fewer."

No one said anything, but the others seemed to agree.

Then Simon said, "Well, what Mr Sharp and I did wasn't exactly *ethical* either. We went to the studio he shares with Al and looked around in Al's office."

"Oh, so Mr Sharp has been *sneaking* around too. I feel a little bit better now," Sarah said.

"What did you find out?" Justin asked.

"This Al *guy* is definitely still a *suspect*," Simon began. He continued to tell the others about the drawing that he and Mr Sharp found in Al's *rubbish bin*. He explained that Al might be trying to sell The Sneakers' song himself.

"But Mr Sharp is his friend!" Kevin said. "He wouldn't steal our song just to make some extra money ... would he?"

"Well, he had a lot of *bills* in his office," Simon said. "Maybe he's got money problems. Maybe he thought he could secretly make some money with our song."

"How do you plan to find out whether it was really him or not?" Julia asked.

"Mr Sharp invited Al to come to the school after lessons are over. He told Al that he had to talk to him about something, but didn't have time to go to the studio. That's when Mr Sharp will show Al what we found and make him *confess*," Simon said. "Will you all be here this afternoon? We should all be here together."

"I won't be here," Julia said.

"Why not?" Sarah asked.

"Because I have to finish what Kevin started. I have to finish our plan because mister lover-boy here *messed* everything *up*."

"What do you mean?" Justin asked.

Kevin was trying not to look at the other band members. He was extremely *embarrassed*. Yes, he liked Susie. But he didn't want the others to know that that had stopped him from learning the truth.

"Can't we talk about this later?" Kevin asked quietly.

"I think the others should know what happened, Kevin," Julia said. Then she told the others what happened between Kevin and Susie.

"We still don't know whether Susie is *innocent*," Julia added. "Kevin didn't get a chance to check other rooms of the house. So I have to go there this afternoon and search through the house myself."

"Whoo, Kevin," Simon *teased*. "It looks like you've found yourself a little girlfriend. I hope your heart doesn't get broken if you find out that she's the person that made us lose five thousand pounds and a *recording contract*."

"Come on, Simon. She's really nice. I don't believe that she did it," Kevin said.

After her last lesson ended, Julia left the school quickly. She wanted to see when Susie arrived at her house.

While Julia was walking home, the rest of The Sneakers came together in room 363. They found Mr Sharp waiting for them there.

"Al will be here in a few minutes," Mr Sharp said. "But when he gets here, let me do the talking first, okay?"

The teenagers agreed.

"Oh, I also wanted to tell you that I called the people that own the website that *released* 'Secret'. They said that the person who put it there used the name Ice123 – and there's no way to find out what the real name is. But at least I made them remove the song from their website," Mr Sharp added.

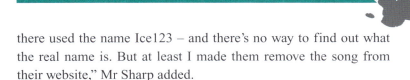

Übung 42: In diesem Textabschnitt sind die Verben durcheinander gekommen. Finde heraus, wohin sie tatsächlich gehören!

Several minutes later they (1. talk) _____ a head covered with grey hair come through the door. The head was (2. belonged) _____ by a big, round belly. The head and the belly (3. saw) _____ to Al.

"Hey Sam, how are you (4. let) _____?" Al said. "Oh, look – you've got your *pint-sized* punk rockers with you too. How are you doing, kids? How's the band?"

"(5. followed) _____ in, Al," Mr Sharp said. "There's something that I ... that we would like to (6. doing) _____ to you about."

"Good. There's something I'd like to say to you too," Al said. "But I'll (7. come) _____ you go first. What I have to say is a bit of a surprise."

"We've got a surprise for him too," Simon said quietly to Kevin. Kevin smiled.
"*What's up?*" Al asked.

"I don't know how to say this to you, Al. This is what's up," Mr Sharp said as he reached into his pocket. He pulled out the drawing he and Simon found in Al's office and unfolded the piece of paper. As he did so, The Sneakers watched Al's face carefully to see if his expression changed. And it did change. The friendly smile on Al's face slowly turned into a look of surprise. Then he looked sad. And finally, the expression on Al's face showed that he was angry.

"How did you get that?" Al asked. "What's happening here? Have you been *sneaking* around in my office? I thought we were business partners! I thought we were friends!"

"Yes, Al. But I don't think a friend would try to *ruin* another friend's project. I don't think my friend would try to steal something from a group of good, hard-working, talented young people."

It seemed that Al didn't know what to say for a moment.

"I don't know what you mean. I was trying to help you," Al said.

"That may be true, Al," Mr Sharp said. "But you should have asked me before you put The Sneakers' song on the Internet. I would have told you not to do it because the band wanted to take part in a *competition*. But one of the rules of the *competition* was that their song couldn't be *released* until after the *competition* was over. And not only that. It also seems that you wanted to try to sell their song yourself. You even designed a CD *cover*. You can't wait to make some money with these kids, can you?"

Übung 43: Formuliere die Sätze in indirekter Rede!

1. "I hate potatoes." Julia said *she hated potatoes*.

2. "I don't want to." Justin said _____.

3. "Where is it?" Sarah asked _____.

4. "Come in, Al." Mr Sharp told _____.

5. "What is Al doing?" Mr Sharp asked _____.

6. "He is a strange *guy*." Kevin said _____.

7. "I think Al did it." Simon said _____.

Al looked as though someone had hit him in the face. His eyes and his mouth were wide open.

"Internet? I wanted to sell the song? What on earth are you talking about, Sam? What have these kids been telling you?" Al asked.

"We didn't have to tell him anything," Simon said. "We found the drawing in your office. And we saw all the *bills* you've got there too. Tell the truth. You wanted to get *publicity* for the band by putting the song on the Internet – and then you wanted to start selling it!"

"I still don't know what you're talking about with this Internet thing," Al said. "Sam, I'd never try to make money through a band that you've been working with. I never have and I never will. You said you were helping the kids with a *competition*. And I could hear that they've got talent. So I wanted to help. Yes, I designed a CD *cover*. But it was going to be a surprise. That's what I wanted to tell you today. I wanted to say that if you win the *competition*, I've already got a great design for your first CD!"

Then Al reached into his *briefcase* and pulled out a large piece of paper. On it was a cool drawing of two burning *sneakers*. Above the flames was written 'The Sneakers'. It looked fantastic!

"I didn't know what the name of your song was, so I left that out," Al said. But now there wasn't much enthusiasm in his voice. He just sounded sad and tired.

"But I guess you don't want my help. You just think I'm a poor old *dope* who only cares about money, don't you?"

Mr Sharp and the band members were *embarrassed*.

"You mean you had nothing to do with the song being put on the Internet?" Sarah asked.

"I really don't know anything about it. Does that mean there's no way that you can win the *competition* now?" Al asked.

"I'm not sure," answered Mr Sharp. "But the most important thing right now is to find out who really did it."

"Do you have any other *suspects*?" Al asked.

"Well, Julia is *investigating* something at this moment," Justin said. "And Simon still hasn't found his copy of the song. But we don't know where it might be or who might have taken it."

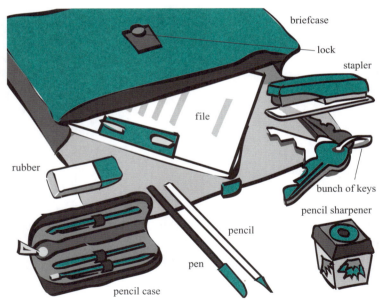

Mr Sharp was right. At that moment, Julia was watching Susie arrive at her house. After Susie went inside, Julia waited a few minutes. Then she went outside and walked over to Susie's front door. She knocked three times. Moments later the door opened.

"Hi, Julia," Susie said. "*What's up?*"

"Hi, Susie. I wanted to know if I could *borrow* something from you.

"Of course. Come in," Susie said.

Julia stepped into the house. She could hear Susie's dog *barking* somewhere in the house. As soon as she got inside, she looked around quickly. On the small table next to the door she saw some keys, a pen, a pencil, and a small black *pencil sharpener*. As Susie was closing the door and looking in the other direction, Julia took the *pencil sharpener* from the table and put it in her pocket. When Susie turned around, Julia smiled at her. Julia was quite nervous, but she didn't want to show it.

"What do you need to *borrow*?" Susie asked. She seemed to be friendly. But she could just be acting, Julia thought.

"I have to finish an art project. But I just realized that I left my *pencil sharpener* at school. Do you have one that I could *borrow*?"

"Certainly," Susie said. She moved to the small table next to the door. But when she looked at the table she *frowned*.

"That's strange," Susie said. "I got home a few minutes ago – and I'm sure that I put my *pencil sharpener* right here. I must have put it somewhere else. Let me look for it. I'll be right back."

"I'll come and look with you," Julia said quickly. "If that's okay."

"Yeah. Come on. Maybe it's in the living room."

Übung 44: Schreibe die Wörter in Großbuchstaben um!

1. Take a letter away from STRANGE to make a word that means 'unusual'. _____

2. Add a letter to PAL to make a word that describes something white or light-coloured. _____

3. Change a letter in FLAKE to make a word for the fire you see on a candle. _____

4. Change a letter in TIMED to make a word that describes someone who has no energy. _____

5. Change a letter in PAIL to make a word for two of something. _____

6. Add a letter to PEAK to make a word for what you do when you say something. _____

Julia followed Susie through the living room. As they walked around the room, Susie looked for her *pencil sharpener*. Julia, however, spent the time looking for her copy of The Sneakers' song. She looked in drawers and under the sofa.

"Why would my *pencil sharpener* be under the sofa, Julia? You have some strange ideas," Susie said.

Soon Susie gave up on looking in the living room.

"Let's try my bedroom. I was up there a second ago," Susie said.

The two girls started going up the stairs.

"Now I can search her room objectively," Julia thought. "Silly Kevin. But I'll make sure that I search every corner of her room."

But about halfway up the stairs Susie stopped.

"Wait! It's probably in the kitchen. I think I put it there!"

She turned around and went back down the stairs. Julia didn't know what to do. She couldn't go up to Susie's room alone. She looked up to the top of the stairs one last time. Then she *sighed* and followed Susie to the kitchen.

In the kitchen Susie continued searching. But Julia wasn't interested in looking any more. She was sure that if Susie had the CD, it was probably in her room. Susie wouldn't keep the CD in the kitchen. Instead of searching with Susie, Julia said hello to the dog, Hunter, who was lying on a big pillow near the oven.

"Hi there, Hunter," Julia said as she rubbed the dog's head. "Hunter is really quiet today, isn't he?"

"Yeah," Susie said. "He's been lying there all day. I think he's got something under his pillow. Some secret little thing he found a few days ago. He won't let anyone see it. I'm just afraid that it's a dead animal. How *disgusting*!"

Julia laughed and said to the dog, "You've got something special under there? What is it? Susie doesn't want you to keep *disgusting* things under there. What have you got?"

She tried to move the dog off the pillow. But he didn't want to move. Then she saw a ham sandwich on the kitchen table. It must have been Susie's after-school *snack*. Julia took a small piece of ham from the sandwich. Then she held the meat in front of the dog's nose.

"Come here, Hunter. I've got something for you," she said.

Übung 45: Übersetze die Wörter und trage sie ins Kreuzworträtsel ein!

1. Haut
2. seltsam
3. Suche
4. Küche
5. verärgert
6. Bleistift

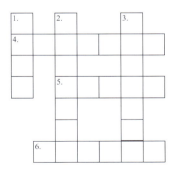

The dog stood up and followed Julia's hand that was holding the ham. As soon as the dog moved away from the pillow, Julia dropped the meat and let Hunter eat it. Then she picked up the pillow.

On the floor was something flat, round and silver. It was a CD! Julia looked closer. She saw handwriting on the CD. She read the letters 'The Sne', and under that she read 'Secr'. The rest of the text was gone. It looked as though Hunter had been playing with and scratching the CD. It was Julia's copy of The Sneakers' song!

"What does Hunter have under there? Did you find something?" Susie asked. She was on the other side of the room and couldn't see what Julia was doing.

As fast as she could, Julia put the CD in her pocket. Then she took the small black *pencil sharpener* out of her pocket and put it on the floor. She stood up.

"Look!" Julia said. "I've found your *pencil sharpener*!"

"What's it doing there? Hunter, you're a bad dog. Don't steal my things!" Susie picked up the sharpener and gave it to Julia.

"Here you go," Susie said.

"Oh, right. Thanks," Julia said. She was so excited about finding the CD that she had forgotten that she asked to *borrow* the sharpener from Susie.

"I've got to go now, Susie," Julia said and left the house quickly. Kevin was right! Susie didn't steal the CD from the hole in Julia's garden. Hunter must have found it and thought it was a toy.

When Julia arrived at room 363 a little while later, she found the other four band members and Mr Sharp in there. But she didn't see Al anywhere.

"What happened to our main *suspect*?" Julia asked. "Where's Al?"

"Al isn't our main *suspect* any more – Susie is. Did you find the CD there?" Justin asked.

"Susie didn't do it. Her dog took the CD from my garden. Here it is," Julia said and pulled out the dirty, scratched CD.

Übung 46: In jedem Satz steht ein Wort an der falschen Stelle. Verschiebe es mit einem Pfeil an die richtige Stelle!

1. I you will give a present for your birthday.
2. I want to go to the concert, but I'm not sure where is it.
3. Why you did decide to do that?
4. There were other no people on the empty street.
5. I'll tell you what do you should.
6. Susie didn't from steal the CD the hole.

"What? But Al is *innocent* too," Simon said. "He was trying to help us by making a design for a CD *cover* for us. He knew nothing about the song being on the Internet. He didn't do it."

"That's just great," Sarah said sadly. "That means we have no *suspects* left. What do we do now?"

"I'll tell you what you should do," Mr Sharp said. "You should all go home and get some rest. All of us have had several very hectic days. Why don't we relax for a while and think about our next step tomorrow?"

Although The Sneakers wanted to find out who was really behind all this, they all agreed. "Hey, I know a great way that we can relax and forget about all this for a while. Why don't we go down to the music shop on Wood Street?" Julia said. "Looking through all those great albums always relaxes me. And it helps to remember that so many other bands have become successful. It gives me hope that we might do it too."

The other band members agreed with Julia's idea.

"Okay, see you all tomorrow, then," Mr Sharp said. "Bye!"

The Sneakers left the school and started walking down the street together. When they walked around a corner, the band members saw Sarah's friend – or ex-friend – Karen.

"Um, I'll see you *guys* later. I've got to talk to Karen," Sarah said.

"Okay, you know where we'll be if you want to meet us later," Simon said.

Sarah didn't know exactly what she wanted to say to Karen. Should she tell Karen the truth? Should she tell her that she took Karen's computer while Karen was swimming? Or should she just tell Karen that she was sorry about everything and wanted to be friends again?

"Hi," Sarah said quietly to Karen.

"Hey," Karen answered.

"Listen, I have to tell you something. I'm really very sorry about the way I've been *behaving*. You've always been a really good friend to me. And I know that I've been spending more time with the band than I have with you. I also understand why you were angry that I wouldn't tell you anything about the band."

"I'm glad to hear that," Karen said.

> **Übung 47:** Unterstreiche die sieben Adjektive, die nicht in den Text passen!

"I had to keep everything about the band a stupid secret. But it seems that I don't have to do that any more. Our hungry chance of becoming successful and famous is gone now. So I guess now I can tell you about what I've been doing." Sarah then told Karen all about the boring *competition*, the *competition*'s special rules, the website where someone had put the song, the missing CDs, and the futuristic *investigations*. However, Sarah didn't yet tell her that she and Justin had broken into Karen's wet *locker* and searched through her lonely computer for *clues*.

Before Sarah got a chance to explain about that, Karen said, "*Speaking of* missing CDs, you can have this back." As she said this, Karen reached into her empty rucksack and pulled out a CD case.

It was the Michael Jackson CD case! But what was inside?

"I've been carrying it around in my rucksack since the day I took it from your room. I know it's really mine, but I don't think I'll ever listen to this kind of music again. Do you want to keep it, Sarah?"

"Yes, yes, yes!" Sarah was almost jumping with happiness.

"Wow, I didn't know you liked Michael Jackson so much," Karen said. "Playing with your band really has changed you, hasn't it?"

Sarah tried to control herself and said, "Oh, I … I'm just happy because this is like a sign that we're friends again. Don't you agree?"

"Hmm … let me think," Karen said. "Yeah, I think I can forgive you. At least you'll have more time for me again."

"Great," Sarah said. But she was starting to feel very *curious*. Was The Sneakers' CD still inside the case? She opened the case slowly, trying not to let Karen see what she was doing.

The CD was still there!

"Hey, that's not my Michael Jackson CD!" Karen said. She had seen the CD inside the case. "What is that? Let me see!" Karen took the CD from Sarah.

Sarah let Karen have it. Sarah *sighed*, and thought that now she would have to tell Karen the whole truth. She'd have to explain that Karen had been a *suspect* for a while. But before she had a chance to begin explaining, Karen said something very surprising.

"Wait a second. The CD says 'The Sneakers'. I've seen a CD exactly like this before. Where did I see it?"

"Yes, tell me – where did you see it?!" Sarah asked excitedly. Karen thought for a moment.

"I know! I saw it in the CD shop on Wood Street. You know, the shop called Music 4 U," Karen said.

"What? They were selling this CD at the shop?" Sarah asked.

"No, it wasn't for sale. I saw it near the *cash register*. I think the *guy* who works there was listening to it. Have you ever seen that *guy* before? I think he's in a heavy metal rock band. He's totally *bizarre*. He wears a long, black leather coat all the time – when it's cold, when it's hot … always. And what a strange-looking face he has."

"Oh my God! That *guy*?" Sarah shouted in shock. "Karen, I'm really sorry, but I've got to go." Karen looked sad.

"Okay, I see." she said, "You have to go back to your 'real' friends now. See you whenever." Karen started walking away, but Sarah stopped her.

! *Übung 48: Wofür stehen die Slang-Kürzel?*

1. 4 U _____

2. R U OK? _____

3. thx _____

4. 2day _____

5. b4 _____

6. pls _____

"Listen, Karen, I promise I'll explain everything soon. I'll tell you the whole truth. You might not like it, because I've done something bad to you. But if we're going to stay friends, I have to tell you – only not now. Please believe me. There's something I have to do now. It can't wait. I'll call you tonight!" Sarah *hugged* Karen and started running down the street in the direction that the other band members had gone.

Sarah ran as fast as she could. She ran down the street but couldn't find them. She turned onto River Avenue, but The Sneakers weren't there. As she ran, she tried to understand why the strange *guy* took their song and put it on the Internet.

"Karen said he's in a heavy metal rock band," Sarah thought. "Maybe his band took part in the *competition* too. And when he found out that we were also in the *competition*, he made it impossible for us to win!"

Then Sarah ran down Wood Street. Finally she reached the music shop, Music 4 U. Through the window she saw Simon, Justin, Julia and Kevin inside the shop.

She also saw the strange *guy* with the black leather coat. He was standing near the window. He was behind the *cash register*, at the front of the shop. A man was standing next to him – probably the shop manager. The *guy*'s back was facing the window. Sarah looked over the *guy*'s shoulder through the window and saw a CD on the table next to him.

It was The Sneakers' CD!

Sarah threw open the door to the shop and ran inside. First she went over to her friends. Before she started talking, she looked back at the *guy* in the leather coat. He seemed surprised and a bit worried. It looked as though he were counting the number of people in their group.

"*Guys*, I have to tell you something," Sarah *whispered*. "I think I know who put our song on the Internet!"
"Who?" the others asked at the same time.

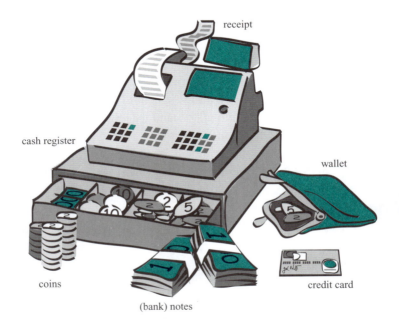

"He did it!" Sarah said and *pointed to* the strange *guy*. When the *guy* saw Sarah pointing to him, he jumped. He turned to the man next to him and said something quickly and quietly. Then he picked up the CD on the table and ran out of the shop.
"See! I told you he did it!" Sarah said. "Now he's trying to get away! Let's get him!"
The five band members ran out of the shop. They looked to the left and saw the *guy* running down the street. Luckily he wasn't too far away. But then he got onto a bike that was standing at the next corner.

Übung 49: In diesen Sätzen sind die Wörter durcheinander gekommen. Wie lauten die Sätze richtig?

1. found the *suspect* Sarah the has in shop

Sarah has found the suspect in the shop.

2. do what Sarah's you would in situation?

___

3. you tell would something I like to

___

4. going the how to is *guy* react?

___

5. Karen Sarah information told some important

___

6. him they difficult will questions ask some

___

"Oh, no! Now we'll never be able to *catch* him!" Simon said.
"Maybe you can't – but I can," Kevin said and *pointed to* his skateboard. He put the skateboard on the ground and jumped onto it.
"You've got your *mobile*, haven't you Simon?" Kevin asked.
"Yeah."
"Good, I've got mine too. As soon as I find out where he's going, I'll call you and you can meet me there. Wish me luck!" Kevin said as he *zoomed* away on his skateboard.
Kevin followed the strange *guy* down the street. He followed him when he turned right. The *guy* started riding up a big hill. It was

extremely difficult for Kevin to stay close to him. The distance between them grew larger and larger. When Kevin finally reached the top, he looked down and saw the *guy* at the bottom of the other side of the hill.

"Oh no! This hill is huge," Kevin said to himself. "Well, here we go …" He pushed off the ground with his foot and started flying down the hill. Kevin had never ridden his skateboard down this hill before because it was so dangerous. He was worried that he would lose control and get hurt. Faster and faster he went. Luckily there weren't any cars on the street.

But then Kevin saw a small stone on the street ahead of him. If he hit a stone going this fast, he'd fly off his skateboard and break every bone in his body! At the last second, Kevin moved his feet a little to the right and avoided the stone. Finally he reached the bottom of the hill and started slowing down.

"Thank God I'm still alive!" he said to himself. Then he looked up and saw that the *guy* was quite far away now. The *guy* turned right onto Bridge Street. Kevin went as fast as he could. But when he reached the corner where the *guy* turned, the *guy* was gone!

Slowly Kevin rode his skateboard down Bridge Street. The *guy* was probably in one of the houses or shops in this street. Then Kevin saw a bicycle between a house and an Italian restaurant. The windows of the house were all dark. Kevin looked through the window of the restaurant carefully. A waiter was standing near the door. There were many tables and *booths* inside. But there didn't seem to be any customers.

Kevin was ready to walk away and accept that he had lost the *guy*. But then he saw something move in one of the *booths* in the restaurant. He saw a piece of black leather. The *guy* was there!

Kevin moved away from the restaurant. He called Simon and told him where he was.

Übung 50: Welches Verb gehört zu welchem Objekt? Trage die richtige Nummer in das Kästchen ein!

1. to invite
2. to take
3. to cut
4. to tell
5. to break
6. to order
7. to ride

- [ ] a bone
- [ ] a guest
- [ ] a bike
- [ ] hair
- [ ] a meal
- [ ] a photo
- [ ] a secret

Ten minutes later The Sneakers were standing next to Kevin.
"Let's get him!" Kevin said. The Sneakers went into the restaurant. They ran to the *booth* where the *guy* was sitting and formed a wall so that he couldn't get out.
"Now we've got you," Justin said.
"You can't get away now. You have to tell us everything!" Simon said.
The strange *guy* answered, "Fine, I'll tell you. But it *was supposed to be* a surprise."
"Oh, you surprised us!" Sarah said. "You wanted your band to win the *competition*, so you made it impossible for us to win!"
"What are you talking about?" the *guy* asked.
"Don't *pretend* you don't know what I mean," Sarah said. "If it's not true, why did you run away when we entered the shop?
"She told me that five of her classmates might come into the shop together," the *guy* said. "She said they might want to talk to me. If that happened, I should take the CD and go away. I don't know what the big problem is. She was just trying to help the other people in her band."
"What a minute," Justin said. "Who is 'she'?"

"She's this girl who's been so nice to me. Most girls think I'm too strange. I guess I *scare* them *away* with my clothes and the music I listen to. But she's different. Her name is Julia."

Sarah, Kevin, Simon and Justin turned to look at Julia. They were all shocked.

"What?! You?" Kevin said. "You were angry with ME for *messing* things *up* at Susie's house. But all the time you were the one who was behind it all!"

"I can't believe this," Justin said. "How could you do this to us? Why did you do it, Julia?"

Julia looked like she was going to cry.

"What are you people talking about?" the *guy interrupted*. "That's not Julia."

"Yes I am," Julia said.

"Tell us more about the Julia you know. And tell us your name," Simon said.

"I'm Rick. I met Julia about a week ago. She came into the shop and saw me using my computer. I was writing some text for my website. She started asking me what I knew about computers. I could see that she liked me. She was flirting a lot. You know girls don't normally flirt with me. They see that I look a little unusual, and they don't like that. But I'll tell you the truth. The only reason why I wear these clothes and listen to heavy metal music is because I thought no one would ever be interested in me anyway. I thought if I just *scared* girls *away*, no one would ever be able to break my heart. But Julia is different. She could see right through my dark, hard *shell*. Julia is …"

"Enough about how wonderful this 'Julia' is. Why do you have our CD – and what did she tell you to do with it?" Julia asked.

"She told me that she was in a band, but she didn't tell me the band's name. She said her band *recorded* a song. She wanted to give the other band members a nice surprise by giving the song some extra *publicity* on the Internet," Rick explained.

Übung 51: Sind die folgenden Aussagen richtig? Markiere mit richtig ✔ oder falsch –!

ÜBUNG 51

1. The Sneakers found Rick in an Italian restaurant. ☐
2. Susie told Rick to put the song on the Internet. ☐
3. Rick is angry with a girl called Julia. ☐
4. Rick is good-looking and many girls want to be his girlfriend. ☐
5. Rick has a website. ☐
6. The things Rick said made Julia upset. ☐

"So she told you to steal a CD, and you did it without asking any questions?" Sarah asked sarcastically. "What kind of idiot are you?"

"She said it wasn't stealing because it was her song too. She told me she saw that *guy*," Rick *pointed to* Simon, "put his copy of the song in his rucksack. So she said if I saw him in the shop, I should try to get the CD from his rucksack."

"I see! So that's why you kept *sneaking* up behind me on that day that I was buying CDs in your shop," Simon said. "I had no idea what you were doing. But I knew I didn't like it."

"After I had the CD, everything else was easy. I just put the song on a website where people can *download* songs," Rick continued. "So you must be the other members of her band. You're called The Sneakers, aren't you? I saw the name on the CD."

"Yes, we are The Sneakers. But there's only one Julia in our band – and she's standing right here," Kevin said and *pointed to* Julia.

"That's not Julia," Rick said. "Julia has long, blonde hair. And she always wears dresses. This girl here is wearing trousers. Julia never wears trousers. And this girl here seems a bit *shy*. Julia isn't *shy* at all. She's always saying that she was born to be a star. You know, it's strange – I never thought I would *fall for* a blonde girl who wears dresses. But I guess she really touched my heart. She made me want to be different."

Übung 52: Setze die richtigen Präpositionen ein! *(on, for, out, of, to, at)*

The Sneakers were quiet 1. _____ a moment. They were trying to think 2. _____ who that could be.

"How could we be so stupid? I know who it must be!" Simon said.

All the band members said the name 3. _____ the same time: "Janet!"

Janet had long, blonde hair and always wore skirts and dresses. And Janet loved to say, "I was born 4. _____ be a star!"

"It's unbelievable," Kevin said. "She seemed to disappear after she found 5. _____ that she wasn't in the band. But all that time she's been working 6. _____ a plan *to get her revenge* on us!"

"And she even used my name! What if things had happened differently? I could have got into so much trouble," Julia said.

"I saw her one day outside the music shop," Simon said. "She seemed so happy and friendly. What a big *liar*! She probably wanted extra *revenge* on me because I never reacted when she flirted with me. And I was chosen to be a singer, not her. That's probably why she decided to steal my copy of the song. I *bet* she used Julia's name because Julia was also chosen to be a singer in the band."

"Wait, you mean she's not in a band?" Rick asked. "And her name is Janet? This is horrible. I was planning to ask her to be my girlfriend. Now I don't even know who she is!"

"Janet lied to all of us. She only wanted *revenge*. She's so *evil*," Justin said.

*Übung 53: Vervollständige die Sätze mit **been**, **gone** oder **went**!*

1. "Where's the *guy*?" "He's _____ into the restaurant."

2. Where have you _____ ? I've been waiting here for hours!

3. I can't find my money anywhere – it's _____ !

4. "Do you want to go to the music shop?" "No, I've already _____ ."

5. I _____ to school yesterday, but I didn't go today.

6. He _____ with them to the concert.

7. We've never _____ to London, but we'd like to go.

Rick started to look worried.
"Hey, I didn't mean to do anything bad, you know," he said. "I just thought I was helping a *cute* girl. I thought she saw the real me – not just my long hair and my leather jacket. She was so nice to me. I hope I didn't make any problems for you."

"Yes, we've got some very big problems because of you and your little friend 'Julia'. But now you're coming with us, Rick. We have to find Janet and make her pay for what she's done," Sarah said.

"We should tell Mr Sharp too," Kevin said. "Does anyone know his *mobile* number?"

No one did. So instead of finding Janet *right away*, they decided to wait until the next day, at school. They told Rick to meet them at their school at noon.

The next morning, Simon found Janet in the corridor at school. He told her to meet him in room 363. He *pretended* to flirt with her and said, "I've got an exciting surprise for you."

Janet loved surprises. She also loved it when Simon showed interest in her. So when the bell rang at noon, she went directly to room 363. The Sneakers were waiting for her. They had told Mr Sharp what happened earlier that morning. So he was with The Sneakers when Janet arrived.

As she opened the door she said, "I'm ready for my surprise, Si…" She wasn't able to finish saying Simon's name. She was too shocked.

"What's going on here? Is this some kind of class *reunion*?" she asked. She tried to bring a smile to her face. But The Sneakers could see that she was nervous.

"No, Janet. It's a special surprise for you," Sarah said. "We," she *pointed to* the rest of the band, "are part one of the surprise. And here is part two."

Sarah *pointed to* Mr Sharp's desk. From behind the desk Rick stood up.

"Hello Julia. Or should I say Janet?" Rick said.

"What are you doing here, *sweetie*?" Janet asked in a false, friendly voice. She went to Rick and put her arms around him.

"Get your hands off me, you *liar*," Rick said angrily. "You used me. You played with my feelings. You made me believe that you liked me, but you only wanted to do something bad to these people here." He *pointed to* The Sneakers.

"What are you talking about, *darling*?" Janet asked. But everyone could hear the worry in her voice.

"That's not all," Kevin said. "You also made it impossible for us to win the band *competition* that we took part in. You stopped us from winning five thousand pounds and a *recording contract* with a big English record company."

"How did you find out that it was against the rules to *release* the song before the *competition* ended?" Justin asked.

Übung 54: Welcher Satz enthält die richtige Zeitform? Kreuze die richtige Lösung an!

1. Ihre Augen zeigten, dass sie nervös war.
   a) ☐ Her eyes have shown that she has been nervous.
   b) ☐ Her eyes showed that she was nervous.
   c) ☐ Her eyes show that she was nervous.

2. Ich freue mich darauf, die Wahrheit herauszufinden.
   a) ☐ I'm looking forward to discovering the truth.
   b) ☐ I'm being looking forward to discovering the truth.
   c) ☐ I will look forward to discovering the truth.

3. Janet wird die Wahrheit nicht länger verbergen können.
   a) ☐ Janet wouldn't be able to hide the truth any longer.
   b) ☐ Janet wouldn't have been able to hide the truth any longer.
   c) ☐ Janet won't be able to hide the truth any longer.

4. Er hat eine gute Idee gehabt.
   a) ☐ He had had a good idea.
   b) ☐ He has had a good idea.
   c) ☐ He have had a good idea.

5. Sie würde es machen, wenn sie es machen könnte.
   a) ☐ She would do it of she could have done it.
   b) ☐ She would do it if she could do it.
   c) ☐ She would have done it if she could do it.

Finally Janet gave up. She stepped away from Rick, and her smile turned into a *sneer*. The friendliness went out of her eyes, and only hate was left.

"You're all such idiots. You thought you were keeping things so secret. But all I had to do was put my ear to the door of room 363 a few times. You *guys* talk loudly – I heard everything. It was simple."

"I remember the day that I heard a noise at the door," Simon said. "You all said I was crazy – but I was right!"

"*What about* me?" Rick asked.

"*What about* you? Nothing. You were an easy *target*. Look at you. You're a *freak*. But I knew you would do anything I told you to do. So I told you to take the CD and put the song on the Internet. How could I really like you? The only boy I've ever liked has been Simon. But when he was chosen to be in the band, he left me behind. He let me fall into a forgotten world while he went on to become rich and famous. But I was born to be a star!" Janet said all of this very dramatically, as though she were acting on a stage.

The Sneakers looked at Mr Sharp.

"What happens now, Mr Sharp? We can make her pay for what she's done, can't we?" Justin asked.

Mr Sharp thought for a moment.

"I'm not really sure, *guys*," he said. "She didn't really break the law. She didn't even steal the CD – she made Rick do it for her. And it's legal to put a song on the Internet."

"But not if the song doesn't belong to you!" Julia said.

"That's true, Julia. But Rick did that for her too," Mr Sharp said. "I'll have to talk to the headmaster. I'll let him decide whether we need to go to the police or not."

The word 'police' made Janet's eyes open wide.

"P-p-police?" she asked nervously. "I can't go to prison! I'm going to be a star. I can't do that from a prison cell."

"You might not go to prison, Janet. But there's going to be trouble for you," Mr Sharp said. "Come with me. We have to talk to Headmaster Jones."

Übung 55: Übersetze die Wörter und enträtsele das Lösungswort!

1. Polizei _ _ _ _ ☐ _
2. Gesetz _ ☐ _
3. Gefängnis _ ☐ _ _ _ _
4. zerstören _ ☐ _ _ _ _ _
5. Rache _ _ _ ☐ _ _ _
6. Sarkasmus _ _ ☐ _ _ _ _

Lösung: _ _ _ _ _ _

Mr Sharp led Janet out of the room. But before she walked out, Janet looked back at Rick and The Sneakers and sneered.

"See," she said, "you can't become famous without me."

The door closed behind them. The room was quiet for a while.

Finally Sarah said, "That crazy *witch*."

"I only wish there was some way to make her pay for everything that she's done. She *admitted* everything. She said she wanted to hurt us, and she wanted to use Rick to do it," Kevin said.

"Maybe there is a way," Justin said. He reached under a desk and pulled out his high-tech laptop computer.

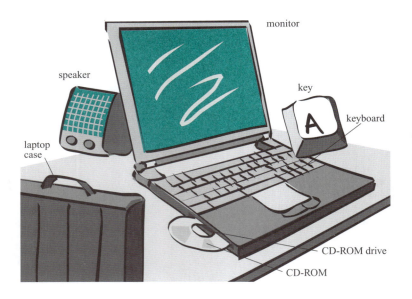

On the *screen* the teenagers could see a row of *buttons* that looked like those on a CD player. The *button* that said '*Record*' was lighter than the others. Justin clicked on the *button* and it turned dark.

"You didn't!" Sarah said happily.

"Oh yes, I did," Justin said with a huge smile. "I *recorded* every word she just said. Listen." He clicked on the 'Play' *button*.

"You're a *freak*. But I knew you would do anything I told you to do. So I told you to take the CD," Janet's voice said. It was coming from the *speakers* on the laptop computer.

Übung 56: Welche Wörter gehören zusammen? Trage die richtige Nummer in das Kästchen ein!

1. money
2. leather
3. business
4. CD
5. pencil
6. ham
7. rock
8. laptop
9. 'Play'

☐ computer
☐ partner
☐ sandwich
☐ coat
☐ problems
☐ band
☐ button
☐ cover
☐ sharpener

The next day was the last day of school before the winter holidays. After this day the pupils would have two weeks without lessons. The bell rang, which marked the beginning of the day's first lesson. But instead of going to their classrooms, The Sneakers went to Headmaster Jones's office. His secretary, Mrs Miller, was sitting outside the office. On the desk in front of her were a lot of papers. There was also a microphone. The microphone was *connected* to *speakers* in every classroom in the school. Mrs Miller used the microphone to make important *announcements* to all the teachers and pupils. But today the microphone would be used to make a different kind of *announcement*.

Simon, Sarah, Kevin and Julia ran up to Mrs Miller's desk.

"Mrs Miller, Mrs Miller! Come quickly!" they shouted. "Someone is smoking in the girls' toilet."

Mrs Miller's face darkened. She was an angry old woman, and the thing she hated the most was smoking. Every time she saw a pupil smoking cigarettes, she looked like she wanted to kill them.

"Well, we'll have to stop that right now," she said furiously. "Headmaster Jones is in a meeting, so I'll have to stop it myself. Let's go, children."

The four teenagers led Mrs Miller down the corridor, and away from her desk. Justin, who had been watching everything, went to the desk as soon as he saw the others leave. He opened his laptop computer and turned it on. He put the computer on the desk. He pressed the 'On' *button* on the microphone. He heard a noise come from the *speaker* on the wall of the office. Then he clicked the 'Play' *button* that was on his computer *screen*.

"You're a *freak*. But I knew you would do anything I told you to do. So I told you to take the CD and put the song on the Internet. I can't go to prison! I'm going to be a star. I can't do that from a prison cell. You can't become famous without me!"

> ! Übung 57: *Unterstreiche im folgenden Textausschnitt die Gegenteile der vorgegebenen Wörter!*
> *(1. quietly, 2. whispering, 3. normal, 4. start, 5. up, 6. worst, 7. smallest, 8. slowly, 9. poor, 10. positive)*

Justin could hear Janet's voice loudly through the *speaker* on the wall. When she said those things yesterday, she was almost screaming. Her voice sounded crazy!

When the recording was finished, Justin clicked 'Stop'. Then he turned off the microphone and ran out of the room with his computer. As he ran down the corridor, he could hear loud laughter coming from every classroom.

It worked! Everyone was laughing at Janet. That was the best way to *punish* Janet for what she'd done. Janet believed that she was a star. But The Sneakers turned her into the school's biggest joke!

As Justin ran past the girls' toilet, he heard the door open. Quickly he ran into the boys' toilet. He could hear Mrs Miller's voice coming from the corridor.

"Who did that? What's happening?!" she shouted as she ran towards the headmaster's office.

Justin put his head out into the corridor. There were Kevin, Simon, Julia and Sarah.

"Great work, Justin!" Julia said.

"Yes, that was perfect," Simon said. "People will be laughing at Janet for a long, long time!"

They all came together for a big group hug.

When they separated, Julia said, "But that still doesn't change the fact that we can no longer win the *competition*. We broke one of the rules."

"I guess our dreams of becoming rich and famous are over," Kevin said.

"Hey, don't be so negative. You never know what's going to happen," Simon said.

The winter holidays were fun and relaxing for all the band members. Julia, Simon, Justin, Kevin and Sarah enjoyed the two weeks without lessons. Although they were all very sad that they could no longer take part in the national band *competition*, they were happy that they had found out who put their song on the Internet.

When they returned to school, they felt fresh and ready to make a new start. When it was time for their music lesson with Mr Sharp, the pupils met again in room 363.

"Welcome back, everyone," Mr Sharp said. "I hope you enjoyed the holidays. It's good to see you all again. But before we start, there's something I'd like to tell you …"

Before Mr Sharp had a chance to continue, the door opened and Headmaster Jones walked in.

"Sorry for *interrupting*," the headmaster said, "but I'd like to make a short *announcement*. Janet Starr will not be returning to this school. She was so *embarrassed* by what happened last month that she asked her parents to transfer her to another school. I only wish we knew who did that."

The pupils smiled nervously.

Übung 58: Finde für das Wort in Klammern ein Reimwort, das in den Zusammenhang passt!

"I'll let you get back to (1. perk) _____ now. Have a nice (2. way) _____," Headmaster Jones said and left.

"I don't know for (3. pure) _____ what happened that day either," said Mr Sharp. "And I don't think I want to (4. though) _____. So I won't ask. Let's just leave all that behind us. But now I'd like you to (5. play) _____ hello to a special guest for our first lesson of the (6. beer) _____. Let me introduce a man who has a lot of experience in the music business. He works with all sorts of (7. hands) _____ at a recording studio. Everyone, say hello to Al!"

The (8. bore) _____ opened and in walked Mr Sharp's partner, Al. The pupils clapped.

"Hi, Al!" Sarah said. "It's good to see you again."
"It's great to see you too," Al said.

"Al is here today to give you a few tips about becoming famous in the music world," Mr Sharp said.

"That's right," Al said. "You might not know it, but I've helped several bands get *recording contracts* with important record companies. So here's tip number one for making your band rich and famous. You should always have two managers. That way you can be sure that one person isn't controlling everything. Take, for example, Sam – I mean, Mr Sharp – and me. We'd be perfect together. We work well together and we'd never try to steal money from each other." Al smiled.

"Tip number two. You need a cool, fun name," Al said and picked up a piece of *chalk*. He wrote on the *blackboard* 'T-H-E S-N-E-A-K-E-R-S'.

"Here's a really good example of a fantastic band name," he said. The band members smiled.

"Tip number three. You need a great song." He pulled a CD out of his pocket. It was Simon's copy of The Sneakers' song, 'Secret'. The copy that Janet had stolen.

"Number four – a sensational CD *cover* design. I hate to give myself compliments, but I must say that this is a good example," Al said and took a CD case out of his bag. The picture on the *cover* of the case was Al's design – the one with the burning *sneakers* and the band's name on it.

Übung 59: Ergänze die Begriffe!

1. p _ _ c _ of *chalk*

2. _ _ c _ e _ of crisps

3. g _ _ _ s of water

4. _ u _ of coffee

5. _ _ t _ _ e of wine

6. _ _ _ y of The Sneakers' song

7. g _ _ u _ of pupils

"After that it gets a little more complicated," he said. "Some bands would take that one song and try to get a whole *recording contract* from a company. But that's not a very realistic plan. And because you are all quite young, a businessman from a record company might not take you seriously. You could try using your song to take part in a *competition*."

"What's your point, Al?" Simon asked.

"We've already tried to do that. But because Janet and Rick

released our song on the Internet, we're no longer allowed to win the *competition*. There's no hope for us now."

"Wait a minute, Simon. That was not the only band *competition* that exists. Another important thing to remember is that you should always think positively. Try not to be so negative," Al said. "I've got a friend at a record company. He says he likes your song a lot and says he would agree to officially *release* the song 'Secret' as a single."

"Yes!" Kevin shouted and jumped up from his seat. "How much money do we get for that?"

"Slow down, Kevin. Because you're a new band, you won't get any money for it," Al said. "But there's still a way to use the *released* single to become more successful. Mr Sharp and I have been collecting information about other band *competitions*. And we've found one that allows bands to take part using songs that have already been *released*."

"Hooray!" The Sneakers said at the same time.

"It's not going to be easy to win," Al continued. "This isn't just a national *competition* – it's a worldwide *competition*. That means you'll be compared with bands from the USA, Japan, Germany, France – everywhere! But the top three bands in the *competition* will all win a chance to get a *recording contract*."

Übung 60: Übersetze!

1. Österreich _____
2. Schweiz _____
3. Irland _____
4. Großbritannien _____

5. Kanada _____

6. Frankreich _____

7. Italien _____

"That's great, Al!" Justin said. "Thank you so much for helping us to get another chance to *make it big*!"

"It's my pleasure, Justin," Al said. "And here's my last tip of the day as your guest speaker. Never give up. Never accept that your chance for success has been destroyed. Think positively, fight for your dreams – and one day your dreams might become a reality!"

That day, Mr Sharp's pupils were more *obedient* than they had ever been before. They followed every last one of the tips Al gave them. They knew that they had the talent and the enthusiasm to turn their dreams to reality.

THE END

Abschlusstest

Übung 1: Welches Wort ist das „schwarze Schaf"?

1. worries, troubles, interests, problems
2. hope, friend, dream, wish
3. skirt, dress, trousers, hair
4. scream, shout, yell, *whisper*
5. *blackboard*, teacher, desk, sofa
6. table, kitchen, bathroom, cellar
7. mouse, *screen*, *keyboard*, piano
8. animal, cat, dog, hamster

Übung 2: In diesem Gitternetz sind acht Getränke versteckt. Findest du sie alle?

S	O	K	J	U	I	C	E
M	C	O	K	E	E	R	Y
U	O	L	W	I	N	E	J
R	F	T	A	K	P	C	N
T	F	E	T	M	I	L	K
W	E	A	E	H	G	B	O
B	E	E	R	D	Y	I	R
E	W	A	T	E	R	B	O

Übung 3: Wähle das passende Wort für jeden Satz aus und unterstreiche es!

1. Is there some/any information about Mr Sharp's friend, Al?
2. I spent most of my money – I haven't got much/many left.
3. Simon has been taking guitar lessons since/for five years.
4. I want to buy a CD. Could you *borrow*/lend me five pounds?
5. Goodbye! We will see us/each other tomorrow.
6. That was so/such a good concert!
7. I don't know whether their/they're coming.
8. Susie remembered/reminded Kevin to call her.
9. That's Susie's pet dog. It's/Its name is Hunter.

Übung 4: Welche Übersetzung der kursiv markierten Slang-Ausdrücke stimmt? Kreuze die richtige Lösung an!

1. Come on, you've got to *chill out*!
   a) ☐ Komm – du musst dich aufwärmen!
   b) ☐ Komm – du musst dich entspannen!

2. Susie likes Kevin. She thinks he's really *fit*.
   a) ☐ Susie mag Kevin. Sie meint, dass er wirklich gut aussieht.
   b) ☐ Susie mag Kevin. Sie meint, dass er durchtrainiert ist.

3. *What's up*, man?
   a) ☐ Was tut sich so, Alter?
   b) ☐ Was geht nach oben, Typ?

4. They *snogged* in her bedroom.
   a) ☐ Sie haben in ihrem Schlafzimmer geschnarcht.
   b) ☐ Sie haben in ihrem Schlafzimmer geknutscht.

Übung 5: Ordne die Buchstaben zu einem sinnvollen Wort!

1. Julia, Simon, Kevin, Justin and Sarah are members of a (dban) _____.

2. Rick listened to music on his (eahdpnhoes) _____.

3. The Sneakers made their CD in Mr Sharp's (oustdi) _____.

4. If they write more songs, they can make an (bmalu) _____.

5. Justin had a CD (pyrlae) _____ in his laptop computer.

6. They tried to win a contract with a (drrceo) _____ company.

7. In a concert, the singer sings into a (imcroepnho) _____.

Übung 6: Übersetze die Wörter und trage sie in das Kreuzworträtsel ein!

HORIZONTAL
1. Verdächtigte(r)
6. Hinweis

VERTIKAL
1. klauen
2. erschrecken
3. böse
4. Dieb
5. umarmen

Übung 7: In diesen Sätzen werden „False Friends" verwendet. Finde das richtige Wort und trage die entsprechende Nummer in das Kästchen ein!

1. Everyone likes Julia – she's very **sympathetic**.
2. I **will** a brand new bicycle for Christmas.
3. Al is the **chef** of the company.
4. I **became** a pet dog for my birthday!
5. I'm trying to **spare** money to buy a CD player.
6. I got perfect **notes** in my last English test.
7. We bought some **gift** to kill the rat.
8. Turn off the lamp. This room is too **hell**.
9. I think Karen did it – what do you **mean**?

☐ boss
☐ save
☐ think
☐ bright
☐ poison
☐ marks
☐ nice
☐ got
☐ want

Übung 8: Schreibe die Wörter in Großbuchstaben um!

1. Take away a letter from SECRETE to make something you're not allowed to tell anyone. _____

2. Change a letter in REACHER to make the word for someone who works in a school. _____

3. Change a letter in PINK to make the word for the kind of music Sarah likes. _____

4. Change a letter in MOUSE to make the word for a place where people live. _____

5. Add a letter to PORT to make the word for what football and tennis are. _____

Übung 9: Vervollständige die Gegensätze!

1. lost   _ _ _ n _
2. adult   _ h _ l _
3. allowed   _ _ r _ i _ d _ _
4. asleep   _ _ ak _
5. relaxed   _ x _ _ t _ d
6. black   _ h _ _ e
7. up   d _ _ _
8. future   _ a _ t
9. work   p _ _ y
10. possible   _ m _ _ _ _ i _ _ _
11. guilty   _ _ n _ _ _ _ t

Übung 10: Setze die richtigen Präpositionen ein!

1. The Sneakers looked _____ the person who stole the song.

2. Sarah and Justin broke _____ Karen's locker.

3. It didn't take them long to find _____ who the real thief was.

4. They had many problems – but they never gave _____.

5. The band got some important information _____ Rick.

6. _____ the end of the story, The Sneakers were happy.

Lösungen

Übung 1: 1. quickly 2. Slowly (or Quietly) 3. quietly (or slowly) 4. immediately 5. loudly

Übung 2: 1. told 2. said 3. heard 4. asked 5. stepped 6. came 7. smiled

Übung 3: 1. trumpet 2. guitar 3. saxophone 4. violin 5. organ Lösung: piano

Übung 4: 1. the 2. an 3. the 4. a 5. a 6. an

Übung 5: 1. 10.15 am 2. 8.55 pm 3. 3.27 pm 4. 11.10 am 5. 12.00 6. 1.30 pm 7. 8.43 am

Übung 6: 1. blue 2. red 3. orange 4. green 5. white

Übung 7: 1. room 2. music 3. class 4. thin 5. radio 6. lesson 7. flu 8. glad

Übung 8: 1. What 2. Which 3. When 4. Who 5. How 6. What 7. When

Übung 9: 1. a 2. a 3. b 4. b 5. b

Übung 10: 1. Mr Sharp teaches music. 2. Kevin plays the bass guitar. 3. The band could win £5,000. 4. Julia likes jazz music. 5. Justin likes the name The *Fabulous* Five.

Übung 11: 1. girlfriend 2. classroom 3. headmaster 4. weekend 5. skateboard 6. someone 7. fingernail

Übung 12: 1. leg 2. shop 3. wood 4. think 5. bell 6. nose

Übung 13: 1. They're 2. There 3. there 4. their 5. their 6. They're

Übung 14: 1. noise 2. pupil 3. sun 4. pen 5. smile

Übung 15: 1. Sarah has a lot of energy. 2. Do you like this song? 3. Justin likes playing with computers. 4. Why is everything a secret? 5. Janet is not in the band.

Übung 16: 1. fewer 2. any 3. prize 4. tell 5. put on 6. taught 7. until 8. about

Übung 17: 1. A village is smaller than a town. 2. A car is more expensive than a bicycle. 3. An ocean is deeper than a lake. 4. Hip-hop music is cooler than classical music. 5. A tree is taller than a bush. 6. A sofa is bigger than a chair.

Übung 18: 1. They jumped when the balloon exploded. 2. Kevin loved to eat chicken and potatoes. 3. It's nice when the weather is sunny. 4. Not many people are on holiday. 5. She works in a factory. 6. I went to the cinema yesterday.

Übung 19: 1. weather 2. street 3. jeans 4. hand 5. eyes 6. later 7. face 8. name

Übung 20: 1. richtig 2. falsch 3. falsch 4. falsch 5. falsch 6. richtig

Übung 21: 1. soon 2. good 3. get 4. boss 5. marks 6. novel

Übung 22: 1. into 2. up 3. on 4. on 5. on 6. over 7. in

Übung 23: 1. happy 2. sweet 3. new 4. later 5. quickly 6. more

Übung 24: 1. b 2. a 3. b 4. c 5. c

Übung 25: 1. (shoutid) shouted 2. (repeeted) repeated 3. (Sorrie) Sorry 4. (grate) great 5. (heer) hear 6. (gayve) gave 7. (azked) asked 8. (smild) smiled 9. (disapeered) disappeared

Übung 26: 1. word 2. notes 3. day 4. song 5. Internet 6. hands 7. eyes

Übung 27: 1. think 2. find 3. lost 4. took 5. band 6. friends 7. sure

Übung 28: 1. safe/dangerous 2. empty/full 3. rich/poor 4. excited/calm 5. back/front 6. often/seldom

Übung 29: 1. anybody 2. Nobody 3. anything 4. anything/anybody 5. nothing

Übung 30: 1. found/discovered 2. place/location 3. created/made 4. part/piece 5. perfect/ideal 6. path/*trail*

Übung 31: 1. thirty-two 2. first 3. thirteenth 4. half 5. eight thousand three hundred 6. five hundred and two

Übung 32: 1. dead 2. strong 3. normal 4. clean 5. cheap 6. ready

Übung 33: 1. paid 2. left 3. got 4. drove 5. going 6. show 7. explained

Übung 34: 1. grass 2. tree 3. rose 4. bush

Übung 35: 1. Then his mum turned the television off. 2. I think it's some kind of cat. 3. The bank isn't open on Sundays. 4. Justin wanted to go home. 5. There was a party happening.

Übung 36: 1. a 2. b 3. a 4. b 5. b

Übung 37: 1. flat/apartment 2. holiday/vacation 3. lorry/truck 4. lift/elevator 5. *trainer/sneaker* 6. rubbish/garbage

Übung 38: 1. Because there are a lot of *bills* in Al's office. 2. They found it in her *locker*. 3. He hid in the toilet *cubicle*. 4. Two girls almost found him. 5. No, she didn't.

Übung 39: 1. which 2. where 3. it's 4. for 5. surprised 6. danger

Übung 40: 1. lemon 2. smell 3. butter 4. oven 5. egg 6. eat 7. open

Übung 41: 1. away 2. out 3. on 4. up 5. of 6. in

Übung 42: 1. saw 2. followed 3. belonged 4. doing 5. Come 6. talk 7. let

Übung 43: 1. Julia said she hated potatoes. 2. Justin said he didn't want to. 3. Sarah asked where it was. 4. Mr Sharp told Al to come in. 5. Mr Sharp asked what Al was doing. 6. Kevin said he was a strange *guy*. 7. Simon said he thought Al did it.

Übung 44: 1. strange 2. pale 3. flame 4. tired 5. pair 6. speak

Übung 45: 1. skin 2. strange 3. search 4. kitchen 5. angry 6. pencil

Übung 46: 1. I will give you a present for your birthday. 2. I want to go to the concert, but I'm not sure where it is. 3. Why did you decide to do that? 4. There were no other people on the empty street. 5. I'll tell you what you should do. 6. Susie didn't steal the CD from the hole.

Übung 47: 1. stupid 2. hungry 3. boring 4. futuristic 5. wet 6. lonely 7. empty

Übung 48: 1. for you 2. Are you okay? 3. thanks 4. today 5. before 6. please

Übung 49: 1. Sarah has found the *suspect* in the shop. 2. What would you do in Sarah's situation? 3. I would like to tell you something. 4. How is the *guy* going to react? 5. Karen told Sarah some important information. 6. They will ask him some difficult questions.

Übung 50: 1. to invite a guest 2. to take a photo 3. to cut hair 4. to tell a secret 5. to break a bone 6. to order a meal 7. to ride a bike

Übung 51: 1. richtig 2. falsch 3. falsch 4. falsch 5. richtig 6. richtig

Übung 52: 1. for 2. of 3. at 4. to 5. out 6. on

Übung 53: 1. gone 2. been 3. gone 4. been 5. went 6. went 7. been

Übung 54: 1. b 2. a 3. c 4. b 5. b

Übung 55: 1. police 2. law 3. prison 4. destroy 5. *revenge* 6. sarcasm
Lösung: career

Übung 56: 1. money problems 2. leather coat 3. business partner 4. CD cover 5. pencil sharpener 6. ham sandwich 7. rock band 8. laptop computer 9. 'Play' button

Übung 57: 1. quietly/loudly 2. *whispering*/screaming 3. normal/crazy 4. start/ stop 5. up/down 6. worst/best 7. smallest/biggest 8. slowly/quickly 9. poor/rich 10. positive/negative

Übung 58: 1. work 2. day 3. sure 4. know 5. say 6. year 7. bands 8. door

Übung 59: 1. piece 2. packet 3. glass 4. cup 5. bottle 6. copy 7. group

Übung 60: 1. Austria 2. Switzerland 3. Ireland 4. Great Britain 5. Canada 6. France 7. Italy

Lösungen Abschlusstest

Übung 1: 1. interests 2. friend 3. hair 4. *whisper* 5. sofa 6. table 7. piano 8. animal

Übung 2: 1. juice 2. Coke 3. wine 4. milk 5. beer 6. coffee 7. tea 8. water

Übung 3: 1. any 2. much 3. for 4. lend 5. each other 6. such 7. they're 8. reminded 9. Its

Übung 4: 1. b 2. a 3. a 4. b

Übung 5: 1. band 2. *headphones* 3. studio 4. album 5. player 6. record 7. microphone

Übung 6: HORIZONTAL: 1. *suspect* 6. *clue*, VERTIKAL: 1. steal 2. scare 3. *evil* 4. thief 5. hug

Übung 7: 1. nice 2. want 3. boss 4. got 5. save 6. marks 7. poison 8. bright 9. think

Übung 8: 1. secret 2. teacher 3. punk 4. house 5. sport

Übung 9: 1. found 2. child 3. forbidden 4. awake 5. excited 6. white 7. down 8. past 9. play 10. impossible 11. innocent

Übung 10: 1. for 2. into 3. out 4. up 5. from 6. At

Glossar

Abkürzungen im Glossar

AE	*American English*
fam	*umgangssprachlich*
sl	*slang*

to admit	zugeben, gestehen
announcement	Ankündigung
appointment	hier: Termin; Verabredung; Ernennung
argument	hier: Streit; Argument
to assume	annehmen, voraussetzen
attention	Aufmerksamkeit
audition	Vorspielen, Vorsingen
to audition	vorspielen, vorsingen
backstabber *sl*	falscher Fuffziger *fam*
backing singer	Backgroundsänger
to bark	bellen
to be supposed to be	sein sollen
to behave	sich benehmen
to bet, bet, bet	wetten
big mouth *sl*	großes Mundwerk *fam*
bill	Rechnung
bit by bit	Stück für Stück, nach und nach
bizarre	seltsam
blackboard	Tafel
booth	hier: Sitzecke; Bude, Stand; Kabine
to borrow	ausleihen
briefcase	Aktentasche

brilliant	hier: genial, hervorragend; leuchtend
buried → to bury	
to burst, burst, burst	hier: (hinein)platzen; bersten, brechen
to bury, buried, buried	begraben, vergraben
button	Taste; Knopf
to care about something/somebody	sich aus etwas etwas machen/sich für jemanden interessieren
cash register	Registrierkasse
to catch, caught, caught	fangen, erwischen
caught → to catch	
chalk	Kreide
changing room	Umkleidekabine
to check out *sl*	ansehen, auschecken *fam*
chick *sl*	Mädel *fam*, Kleine *fam*
to chill out *sl*	sich entspannen, langsam machen *fam*
chlorine	Chlor
to clap	klatschen
clue	Hinweis
combination lock	Zahlenschloss
competition	Wettbewerb
to confess	gestehen, bekennen
to confuse	verwirren
confused → to confuse	verwirrt, durcheinander
to connect	verbinden
connection	Verbindung, Beziehung
to contact somebody	sich mit jemandem in Verbindung setzen
cover	hier: Cover; Abdeckung; Hülle

crowd	Menge
cubicle	hier: (Einzel)toilette; Kabine
curious	neugierig
cute	süß
damn *sl*	verdammt *fam*
darling	Liebling
disgusting	empörend, widerlich
dope *sl*	Trottel *fam*, Idiot *fam*
to download	herunterladen
to embarrass	in Verlegenheit bringen, blamieren
embarrassed → to embarrass	verlegen
emergency	Notfall
ethical	hier: moralisch einwandfrei; ethisch
evil	böse, schlecht
fabric	hier: Stoff; Gefüge, Struktur
fabulous	fantastisch
fight	Kampf, Streit
file	Datei
fit *sl*	geil *fam*
footprint	Fußabdruck
freak *sl*	Irre(r); Computerfreak
to frown	die Stirn runzeln
geek *sl*	Außenseiter
genius	Genie
to get one's revenge	sich rächen
guy *sl*	Typ *fam*
guys *sl*	Leute *fam*
to hang out *sl*	rumhängen *fam*
headphones	Kopfhörer
to hug	umarmen

I'm gonna be *sl* (I'm going to be)	ich werde … sein
indoor swimming pool	Hallenbad
innocent	unschuldig
insecure	unsicher
to interrupt	unterbrechen
to investigate	untersuchen, nachgehen
investigation	Nachforschung
keyboard	Tastatur; Keyboard
knackered *sl*	kaputt *fam*, geschlaucht *fam*
laid-back	ruhig, gelassen
to let someone down	jemanden im Stich lassen
liar	Lügner(in)
to lick	(ab)lecken
local	örtlich
to lock	verschließen, schließen
locked → to lock	verschlossen, geschlossen
locker	Schließfach, Spind
loo *sl*	Klo *fam*
mega *sl*	spitze *fam*, super *fam*
to melt	schmelzen
melted → to melt	geschmolzen
mobile	Handy
necklace	Halskette
neighbour	Nachbar
to nick	mitgehen lassen
nightmare	Albtraum
no … either	auch nicht, auch kein
obedient	gehorsam
oops *sl*	hoppla *fam*
pavement	Bürgersteig

pencil sharpener	Bleistiftspitzer
pint-sized	winzig, knirpsig
to plug into	einstecken, anschließen an
plugged into → to plug into	angeschlossen an
poetry	Poesie, Gedicht(e)
to point to	deuten auf, zeigen auf
to pretend	vorgeben, so tun als ob
to protect	schützen, beschützen
publicity	Werbung
to punish	bestrafen
to recommend	empfehlen
to record	aufnehmen
recording contract	Plattenvertrag
rehearsal	Probe
to release	herausbringen, veröffentlichen
release	Neuerscheinung
research	(Nach)forschung
reunion	hier: Treffen; Versöhnung, Wiedervereinigung
revenge	Rache
right away	sofort, auf der Stelle
rubbish bin	Abfalleimer
to ruin	ruinieren, zerstören
to scare away	verschrecken
to scratch	zerkratzen
screen	hier: Bildschirm; Leinwand
shaggy	zottelig, zerzaust
to shake, shook, shaken	schütteln
shell	Schale
shook → to shake	
shut up *sl*	halt die Klappe *fam*

shy	schüchtern
to sigh	seufzen
to sneak	schleichen
sneaker *AE*	Turnschuh
sneer	spöttisches Lächeln
to snog *sl*	(rum)knutschen *fam*
so what? *sl*	na und? *fam*
speaker	hier: Lautsprecher, Sprecher
speaking of	da wir gerade von … sprechen
stack	Stapel, Stoß
stuff *sl*	Zeug *fam*
suspect	Verdächtige(r)
sweetie *sl*	Schatz, Süße(r) *fam*
tambourine	flache Handtrommel
target	Ziel
to tease somebody	jemanden aufziehen, necken
thrilled	begeistert
top secret	streng geheim
trail	hier: Spur; Weg, Pfad
trainer	Turnschuh
trust	Vertrauen
van	Lieferwagen, Wagen
vocals	Gesang
what about …?	wie wäre es mit …? was ist mit …?
what the heck …? *sl*	was zum Teufel …? *fam*
what's up? *sl*	was ist los?
to whisper	flüstern
wicked *sl*	geil *fam*
witch	Hexe
youngster	Jugendliche(r)
to zoom	hier: sausen; zoomen